CACTI AND SUCCULENTS

The author of this book, who is Assistant Editor of *Amateur Gardening* and *Gardening Illustrated*, has been growing succulent plants as a hobby for many years, under all sorts of conditions including in the living-room. He is thus familiar with the minor problems which may beset the beginner, and gives concise cultural details for growing these plants in greenhouse, or frame, or on a window-sill. Pests and diseases and their control are fully described, as are methods of propagation.

The chapter on culture is introduced by a description of the adaptations whereby succulent plants resist drought conditions, and the plant forms that have resulted. A short study of the characteristics of the families of succulents leads on to a list in which most of the plants readily obtainable, and their particular needs, are detailed.

An Amateur Gardening Handbook

THIS BOOK

IS NO 3 OF THE AMATEUR GARDENING HANDBOOKS

others in the series are

1. Garden Chrysanthemums

2. Flowering Shrubs

4. Annual Flowers

5. Greenhouse Flowers

6. Roses

7. Greenhouse Chrysanthemums

8. The Beginner's Garden

9. Vegetable Gardening

10. House Plants

11. Lawns

12. Rock Gardening

NEW TITLES ARE ADDED FROM TIME TO TIME

AMATEUR GARDENING HANDBOOK NO 3

CACTI AND SUCCULENTS

A. J. HUXLEY

W. H. & L. COLLINGRIDGE LTD

2-10 TAVISTOCK STREET COVENT GARDEN LONDON WC2

FIRST PUBLISHED IN 1953

The Amateur Gardening Handbooks
are published by
W. H. & L. Collingridge Limited
2-10 Tavistock Street London WC2
and printed and bound in England by
Hazell Watson & Viney Limited
Aylesbury and London

SECOND IMPRESSION 1954

CONTENTS

Introduction   7

1. What succulents are   9
   Water requirements—Other habitats—Heat and humidity—Mechanisms for retention of water—Roots—Leaves—Leafless forms—Adaptability—Collecting succulents—Cristates

2. Cultivation   17
   The greenhouse—Frames—Heating and ventilation—Soil mixtures—The materials—Potting—Plants in bowls—Staging—Plants outside—Watering—Keeping succulents in rooms

3. Propagation   35
   From seed—By cuttings—Grafting

4. Pests and diseases   42

5. The families of succulents   46

6. List of genera   57

Cover illustration: An Epiphyllum hybrid

5

ILLUSTRATIONS

1. Some rosette plants 12
2. Some examples of cristate cacti 16
3. Propagation by cuttings and offsets 38
4. Some shrubby plants of the *Mesembryanthemum* group 51
5. Some highly adapted *Aizoaceae* 52
6. A group of Astrophytums or Star Cacti 60
7. Bryophyllums and Kalanchoës 61
8. A few Crassulas 66
9. *Echinopsis Eyriesii* 69
10. A hybrid *Epiphyllum* 70
11. Some Euphorbias 72
12. Two of the Candle Plants 78
13. *Leuchtenbergia principis* 80
14. Cacti with tubercles 82
15. Members of the *Aizoaceae* 83
16. Different forms of Opuntias 85
17. Another group of much-adapted *Aizoaceae* 87
18. *Ceropegia Sandersonii* and *Stapelia gigantea* 91

INTRODUCTION

IF any apology is needed for the addition of one more to the many works on succulent plants, I would say, first, that in this small, cheap book I believe there is all the information to enable any beginner to grow succulents successfully, as well as a list giving details of 81 genera, including most of those readily available. Secondly, I have tried to put the main families of succulents into proper perspective, not, like so many other works, emphasizing only the *Cactaceae*—not by any means the most attractive or interesting.

These plants are apt to become an absorbing hobby, if not a mania. As due warning, I quote from the late Karel Capek's *The Gardener's Year* (by kind permission of the publishers, Messrs Allen & Unwin) 'On the Cultivators of Cacti':

'. . . There are some cactus-men who believe in powdered marble, whereas others believe in brick-dust, and others in charcoal; some approve of water, while others reject it; there are profound mysteries in a Real Cactus Soil which no cactus maniac would betray, even if you broke him on the wheel. All these sects, observances, rituals, schools and lodges, as well as the wild or hermit cactus maniacs, will swear that only by their Method alone have they achieved such miraculous results. Look at this Echinocactus Myriostigma. Did you ever see anywhere else such an Echinocactus Myriostigma? So I will tell you, on condition that you will not tell anyone else, it must not be watered but sprinkled. That's what it wants.—What! cries another cactus-man. Who ever heard that Echinocactus Myriostigma could be sprinkled? Do you want its crown to catch cold? My dear sir, if you don't want your Echinocactus to die straight away of putrefaction you must damp it only by putting it once a week, with the pot, in soft water, warmed to 23·789° Celsius. Then it will grow like a turnip.—God Amighty! shouts the third cactus-man, look at that murderer! If you damp the pot, sir, it will be covered with Proto-coccus; the soil will get sour, and you will be done for—yes, done for; besides your Echinocactus Myriostigma will rot at the root. If you don't want your soil to turn sour, you must water it every second day with sterilized water, and in such a way that 0·111111 gramme, exactly half a degree warmer than the air, comes on a cubic centimetre.—Then the cactus maniacs begin to shout all together, and attack one another with their fists, teeth, hooves and claws; but as is the way of this world, the real truth is not brought to light even by these means.'

Well, it is not quite as difficult as that; but anyone approaching such a pitch will inevitably seek more specialized works; if my book acts as a stepping-stone to these, I shall be well satisfied.

The keen grower may also like to join one of the two societies devoted to these plants.

My gratitude is due to Miss Dora Ratman, who has packed 57 species into 17 small illustrations, and to Mrs Vera Higgins and Mr Gordon Rowley for their helpful criticisms.

CHAPTER ONE

WHAT SUCCULENTS ARE

MANY families of plants which live in comparatively dry regions have evolved structures to withstand long periods of dryness. Such plants are scientifically known as xerophytes. Many such structures, though not all, can be classed under the heading of *succulence*—the provision of fleshy, water-retaining tissue, often protected in some way from the scorching effect of the sun. Some succulents have lost all their leaves in the process, as in many of the *Cactaceae*; others have reduced their leaves to a single fleshy mass, as in some of the *Aizoaceae*. These two families are almost exclusively succulent, but there are many others in which some members have developed succulence.

Water Requirements Even the most highly specialized succulent plant requires some water, and no plant can live in completely arid deserts. Some do live, however, in desert regions where the annual rainfall is as little as 3 or 4 in., and may be restricted to a single month. This, however, is exceptional, and night temperatures, which may fall to almost freezing-point, provoke heavy dew, which plays a considerable part in the life of such plants. In most deserts, a fairly heavy rainfall is concentrated into a few weeks, while during the rest of the year little or no rain falls.

Other Habitats It must not be thought that succulent

plants inhabit only semi-desert regions. Some of the *Cactaceae,* for instance, live as epiphytes—that is, perched on trees or rocks—in the tropical rain-forests of South America; and many of the others live in the African scrub and jungle.

The conditions in high mountains are basically similar to those in deserts, due to almost equally limited rainfall, drying winds and, often, very limited soil. In winter the ground may be frozen and water is withheld from the plant. The hardy succulents, such as Sedums and Sempervivums, some of which are native to Britain, have been evolved in such conditions.

Salt flats and sea coasts are other places which have provoked succulent plant forms; here water absorption is limited by a high proportion of salt in the water. Our native Glasswort (*Salicornia*) is an example.

The grower of succulents does not usually include the hardy kinds; but this is a rather arbitrary outlook, for hardiness is relative, and some cacti which live on the high plateaux of Mexico, or in the Andes, may be covered in snow during the winter. That they and the other hardy succulents survive in the cold is due to their being dry at these times, and also to the air being very dry.

Heat and Humidity Some of the South African succulents will withstand a soil surface temperature of 140° F. and a relative air humidity as low as 10 per cent. Those species that live in scrub or forest are obviously accustomed to greater atmospheric humidity.

Mechanisms for Retention of Water The structural

mechanisms developed to deal with severe drought conditions are varied and ingenious. They must clearly be devoted (1) to absorbing water quickly when it is available, and (2) to reducing water loss (transpiration) to the minimum. In this way the maximum water is retained in the tissues—sometimes as much as 95 per cent of the plant's volume is water.

Roots Many succulents make very extensive root systems in nature. Those of some plants go very deep to tap a water-table; more usually they spread widely close to the surface, so that the regular dew can be absorbed.

The soil in a desert is not like the loam in our gardens; it consists usually of weathered rock particles, but due to the limited rainfall the mineral salts in it are not leached out rapidly, and it is very fertile indeed when rain permits the plant to make use of it. Another feature of the desert is that it has perfect drainage: no water remains near the surface for any length of time.

Leaves The leaves are almost always protected in some way against the full force of the sun. Often only a thin layer of cells is left to carry out photosynthesis, by which (together with the minerals brought up by the roots) the plant's food supply is produced; the rest of the tissue consists of water-storage cells. The outer skin is usually thick, often coated with wax or with white hairs, which act as an insulating medium and often reflect back sunlight also.

The rosette arrangement of leaves (Fig. 1) is common, since it permits an extensive photosynthesizing surface in the minimum space. Sometimes the leaves in the

1. Some rosette plants. 1. *Haworthia planifolia*; 2. *Agave parassana*; 3. *Aeonium tabulaeforme*; 4. *Aloe variegata*.

rosette can close up to form a bulb-like shape in excessive heat.

More often the leaves tend to diminish in number and size, and to become cylindrical or globular in shape, which reduces the transpiring area in relation to volume. They may be closely pressed to the stem, or in extreme examples the stem is dispensed with and the plant becomes a single, more or less globular body. The leaves may wither and shrink in the dry period, when no growth occurs at all.

Some of these 'plant-bodies' grow so that only the round, flattish top is exposed to the sun. In some curious examples a 'window' is formed at the top. The skin contains a layer of calcium oxalate crystals which reduces the power of the sun's rays but allows sufficient to reach the chlorophyll layer deep inside the plant body.

Leafless Forms This is one extreme: the other is the more or less complete absence of leaves. Most of the cacti are leafless or bear leaves for only a short time, and some other succulents, such as the Euphorbias, are similar. Such plants, known as stem succulents, are thick and fleshy, consisting almost entirely of water-storage cells, with a thin photosynthesizing layer protected by a thick skin—a function of the leaves taken over, as in various other plants, by the stem. They are usually globular or columnar, shapes again which minimize the proportion of surface area to volume. Many stem succulents also shrink in the dry season, to plump out at the first rains.

Of course the minimization of surface area reduces photosynthesis as well as transpiration. Hence the growth of the most highly drought-adapted forms is slow.

Another group accepted as succulents includes plants with normal leaves but which have a swollen or bulbous stem above ground. Ordinary bulbous and tuberous plants, with their swollen parts below ground, are not regarded as succulents, though indeed they are often adaptations to at least a seasonal period of drought. Similar are some trees with swollen stems which store moisture (e.g. *Jatropha*), and *Testudinaria,* a thin climber, has a large swollen stem-base capable of storing moisture for years of drought.

Adaptability From the foregoing it should be clear that the succulents cannot all be treated in the same way. They are, it is true, extremely adaptable and tough, and many will put up with conditions far removed from those of their native habitat. The most difficult are those which, owing to the seasons in their home, have clearly defined resting and growing seasons, which must be followed. Where these seasons do not coincide with ours, these plants may be very hard to grow here.

Where succulents have been introduced to other countries where conditions are to their liking, they have spread enormously, like the well-known Prickly Pear (*Opuntia spp.*), which quickly developed into a pest of terrifying proportions in Australia until means were found to destroy it. Many American succulents, such as cacti and Agaves, thrive in the Mediterranean area, where the climate is perfect for them, growing more rapidly and healthily than in their native homes. Even in the Channel Islands and Scillies, many shrubby Mesembryanthemums, native to South Africa, grow luxuriantly, and a few are widely naturalized on our own south-west coasts.

Collecting Succulents. Succulent plants, long popular in Europe and Scandinavia, became fairly popular in Britain before the war, and since then have become much more so. Though a few people find them ugly, to others their grotesqueness and oddity are attractive, and once one becomes at all familiar with them their bizarre shapes and colourings and often large and brilliant flowers are found to possess a unique interest and beauty.

Many are tough, neglect-resisting, and in particular actually enjoy dry atmospheres; thus they are perfect for a sunny window-sill in the living-room. Moreover, small plants are easily obtained at reasonable cost, and few

14

grow very fast, so that a quite extensive collection can be kept in a small space.

While we must thank the florists for bringing succulents to common notice, some of the plants are certainly difficult to grow, and it is a pity that some florists, who seldom know much about their requirements nor their suitability for room culture or for the inexperienced grower, should now be offering more of these difficult plants for sale. Without knowledge failure is almost certain, and the whole group of succulents may then be dismissed as being too much trouble.

All succulents are frequently referred to as 'cacti', but this is quite incorrect. The *Cactaceae* are one family—admittedly the largest—among many that have succulent members.

CRISTATES

It is fairly common to find various garden plants with a flattened or distorted stem. This is usually due to *fasciation,* a phenomenon in which the growing point of a stem divides and multiplies abnormally, usually due to some accident. Fasciated succulents are known as cristates.

Among succulents, especially cacti, this is very common, and there are a large number of cristate forms, which are sometimes beautiful and always extraordinary. Some cristates develop in one direction only, resulting in a flat fan-like growth which in time becomes convoluted, not unlike coral; in others a vast number of tiny heads is produced, or sometimes the rib and tubercle formation

15

2. Some exam-
ples of cristate
c a c t i . L e f t,
*Opuntia cylind-
rica cristata*;
centre, *Lopho-
cereus Schottii
monstrosus*;
right, *C e r e u s
p e r u v i a n u s
m i n o r m o n-
strosus.*

becomes entirely irregular. Examples of the latter two
are often referred to as monstrosities rather than cristates. The Latin word *monstrosus* or *cristatus* after the
specific name indicates a fasciated variety (Fig. 2).

Cristate cacti are reproduced by grafting or, if suitable, from cuttings; cristate succulents other than cacti
are increased by cuttings. Seed seldom reproduces crista-
tion. An artificial cut or incision will sometimes induce
this formation in a normal plant.

CHAPTER TWO

CULTIVATION

DESPITE all the differences of family and habitat, most succulent plants can be grown in similar soil, temperature and air conditions: they are nothing if not adaptable. To get the best results, with steady growth and regular flowering, the needs of some groups need to be properly studied; but there are few succulents that can be killed so long as the basic essentials are followed.

In our winter especially, the main difference to natural conditions is lack of light. Fortunately, in many cases these plants adjust themselves readily to our seasons, and our winter becomes their resting period. At this time, freedom from frost and considerable if not total reduction of watering are all that is necessary. The imitation of the resting period is the most important aspect of cultivation in Britain. Plants which will not rest in the winter need great care.

Succulents should *not* be put in a cellar or a cupboard in the winter. *They need light.*

The Greenhouse A greenhouse is the best place in which to grow succulents. The best type is a rather low, span-roof house, and if it can be built over a pit so much the better. It should be in a sunny place, and should permit the entry of the maximum amount of light. For this reason large panes are best. Good ventilation is equally essential, for even our relatively weak sun may damage succulents if they are in a stuffy, moist atmosphere; also soft growth may result, liable to rotting in winter. Thus a wide span is desirable, with side, roof and, if possible, wall ventilators.

These are ideal requirements: almost any greenhouse will do. If the house is very small, however, ventilation becomes even more important, as it is so easy for conditions to become stuffy in a short time; also, pots dry out very rapidly if the house gets overheated. Ample provision for fresh air should therefore be made.

Attention should be paid to the floor, so that surplus water drains away freely. A concrete floor, with slight slope into a drainage channel and drain, is to be recommended.

For most plants the usual staging at about waist height is adequate. The usual wooden slats will do, but a solid base on which a layer of small gravel or coarse grit is spread is better, and it is useful to have a section of staging which can be built up to form a bed into which pots can be plunged. This is particularly so with the smaller *Aizoaceae*, as explained later. The latter, and other specialized forms, are best kept 2 or 3 ft. from the glass. A high shelf close to the glass is useful for ripening such plants in their resting period, and also to accommodate plants which hang or trail.

If the main staging can be built of concrete, this is useful, since it will absorb surplus water. If not, then care must be taken that excess water drains away from the solid base.

If very large specimens are in question, they are best

set, either in pots or planted direct, in a prepared bed at ground level.

It is obvious that it is inadvisable to mix succulents and other greenhouse plants, for the latter require far more atmospheric humidity.

Frames   In the absence of a greenhouse a frame can be used, particularly for plants not requiring a high winter temperature. The standard 'English' frame is suitable, 3 or 4 ft. wide, 4 to 6 ft. long, and at least 15 in. deep. As in the greenhouse, large panes are to be preferred. Dutch-lights are perhaps too easily broken; 24 in. square is a good size. Even if there is a greenhouse, a frame is valuable for growing seedlings and harbouring newly rooted cuttings during the summer.

Heating and Ventilation   The greenhouse or frame must have some provision for heating in winter, to maintain a minimum temperature of round 45° F. Continued temperatures below 40° F. are harmful to most succulents, and some, in particular the highly adapted members of the *Aizoaceae*, prefer a higher winter temperature, not above 50° F.: with many such plants the growing period occurs in winter. It is simpler, perhaps, though not in any way necessary, to keep such plants in a separate house or at least well-separated from others. Where lower winter temperatures are desirable, as with some cacti, which flower less freely if not kept cold at this season, this is indicated in the List of Genera.

There are many methods of heating. In a small house the common paraffin heater may be used, with the usual care to prevent fumes, which may damage plants. Hot-water pipes heated by a boiler are standard in many houses, and are quite efficient but tedious to maintain. To my mind, electric tubular heating, controlled by a thermostat, is the ideal. It is relatively cheap to instal though undoubtedly more expensive to run; the thermostat prevents waste, often difficult to achieve with boilers, and there is no maintenance or worry involved. Thermostatically controlled gas heating is also available, and is as reliable and costs roughly as much as electricity.

For the frame, the only suitable method is electric tubular heaters; soil-warming cable does not heat the air appreciably. Since the glass is so close to the plants, temporary covering with sacking, etc., is advisable in really cold weather.

Succulents always like fresh air, and should be given as much as possible, winter and summer, as long as the weather is suitable. In winter, ventilators should be opened by day as long as the required temperature is maintained, and there is no fog or mist. Draughts must be prevented: a cold wind will damage a plant far worse than mere cold. Therefore those ventilators away from the wind must be opened—another reason for having plenty of them.

As spring and summer come on, there will be less need to heat the house; but watch must be kept for sudden cold spells and frosty nights, particularly if a previous warm spell has started the plants into growth. It is here that an automatic heating system scores: the thermostat will cope with the situation which might mean struggling with heater or boiler unexpectedly, and prevent the tragedy of damaged plants if cold has descended unforeseen.

In warm weather the main thing to watch is ventilation. On hot, still days all the vents can be opened. If it is windy those on the windward side are closed, for even in summer draughts should be avoided. Movement of air is necessary though, especially if the weather is damp and the air moist. Our climate is so variable that some closing of vents at night is advisable to guard against a change of wind direction or driving rain.

Mechanisms that open ventilators as the temperature rises can be obtained, and should be valuable, especially in spring and autumn if the house has to be left unattended. Unfortunately they are rather expensive.

Plants in frames should be ventilated in the same way. When the weather is still coldish the frame light may be propped up, the aperture depending on conditions. In high summer the light may be removed altogether, unless 'difficult' plants which might resent excessive rainfall are involved. For most plants, particularly seedlings, the air and undiluted sunlight are very beneficial and result in sturdy, mature growth well able to stand the winter.

Shading Most succulents do not need shading in Britain, though under glass, in very bright weather with no air movement, yellowing or scorching may occur if temperatures go over 80° F. All highly adapted forms need maximum sunlight at all times, and the glass must be kept clean to ensure this. Only a few must be shaded; they include the epiphytic cacti. Where a plant requires shading, this is stated in the List of Genera.

The best means of shading such plants is a thin film of whitewash with a very little linseed oil, on the outside of the glass; commercial materials are too thick.

As our sunlight is weak and infrequent in winter, as much as possible must reach our plants. Therefore the glass should be well washed in autumn, and this should be repeated as and when necessary, particularly in towns where soot soon films the glass.

Soil Mixtures The adaptable succulents can be grown in almost any sort of soil so long as it is porous and properly drained; but a well-balanced mixture will, other things being equal, give better results—steady growth, regular flowering, freedom from disease.

Every authority on succulents gives different soil mixtures, which may recommend various combinations of loam, leaf-mould, cow manure, sand, crushed brick, etc. In these mixtures the proportion of 'soft' substances to 'solid' varies from 1:1 to 2:1. The fact that all these authors have had success with such different mixtures is an indication that the proportions are not critical, as long as the basic principles are kept in mind—porosity, and absence of any fermented material or quick-acting manure or fertilizer.

Reasonable results can be achieved with equal parts of loam and coarse sand, with a little peat; but recent experiments suggest that the standard John Innes potting compost, with extra grit, is as suitable for succulents as it is for other pot plants.

The proportion of soft/solid in this compost is 5:1, which is obviously too high. Below are set out the con-

stituents of the J.I. compost and of the additions to it—
1 part grit to 3 of compost—which are recommended for
succulents, to bring the soft/solid ratio to about 1·6:1.
A good proprietary mixture based on the J.I. formula
may be bought ready-made.

Materials	Standard J.I. Potting Compost	Additions	Recommended Succulent Compost
Medium loam	7	–	7
Horticultural peat	3	–	3
Coarse sand	2	2	4
Crushed brick	–	2	2
Charcoal (small lumps)	–	$\frac{1}{2}$	$\frac{1}{2}$

In addition, the J.I. compost includes a fertilizer, made
from $\frac{3}{4}$ oz. ground chalk or limestone, 2 ozs. hoof and
horn meal (about $\frac{1}{2}$-in. grist) and 2 ozs. superphospate of
lime per bushel of compost. This can be used for succulents, with the addition of about $\frac{1}{2}$ part crushed old
mortar rubble or small limestone chips to the compost;
but it provides a rather high proportion of nitrogen,
which promotes top growth, to phosphorus, which assists
root growth.

As a less growth-promoting fertilizer, the following is
to be recommended: basic slag, 2 parts; bone meal, 4
parts; potassium chloride, 1 part. This may be mixed
with 3 parts chalk or similar material, and the whole
mixed into the compost at the rate of 1 part per 100 of
compost. The potash assists ripening, important especially in this country. Bonemeal may be used alone.

The shrubby members of the *Aizoaceae* can be grown

23

in this mixture, but for the real desert forms the proportion of sand should be increased. The above mixture, with another 4 parts of coarse sand, with some broken brick if desired, is usually quite suitable (i.e. 2 parts grit to 3 parts J.I. compost).

The less succulent jungle-living cacti prefer a higher proportion of organic matter. The peat in the recommended mixture may be increased to 5 parts, and may with advantage be mixed with *well-rotted* leaf-mould.

The Materials Any organic material that is actively decomposing, like insufficiently rotted manure or compost, must be avoided, and since fresh loam may contain fresh organic matter, it should preferably be left for some time in a dry shed before use. It is also best sterilized, to kill insect pests and fungus spores. Good sundriesmen will sell sterilized loam, and will use it in any proprietary mixture. A medium or somewhat clayey loam is best, without too much fibre.

Many authorities recommend leaf-mould, and sometimes cow manure, in place of the peat suggested. If these are used they must also have completely rotted. With cow manure this means leaving it for about a year. Since peat is easier to obtain and may be used immediately, the average amateur may prefer to use this in conjunction with the slow-acting fertilizers recommended above. Granulated horticultural peat should be obtained, not coarse, highly acid moorland peat.

The sand should be really coarse, with only a small proportion of particles less than $\frac{1}{16}$ in. Small gravel or stone chips can be added, as well as crushed bricks from

$\frac{1}{4}$ in. to $\frac{3}{4}$ in. The sand should be clean and not salty; sea sand should not be used unless thoroughly washed.

Potting Succulents need repotting like any other plants, and those that grow rapidly will fill a pot with roots in a year. The most frequent causes of collapse are allowing plants to become so root-bound that there is literally nothing left in the soil, and clogged drainage, both of which are averted by regular repotting.

As with any plant, pots and crocks should be clean and sterile. The essential with succulents is to provide good drainage. The best time to repot most cacti is between March and May; other plants as soon as signs of renewed growth are seen, and preferably when the outside temperature is at least 55°. Succulents *can* be repotted at any time, so long as there is active growth, and if a plant is doing badly the first thing to do is to look at the roots.

Young and vigorous plants may need annual potting, and others are best repotted every two or three years. Slow growers with poor root systems may be left longer. Before repotting, the soil should be fairly dry. Turn the plant out of the pot by holding the stem in one hand, the pot upside down and tapping the rim on the edge of the bench or staging. Holding the plant is not always easy: small, soft plants must be held very gently, and with spiny ones leather gloves should be worn or the stem held in a pair of padded tongs. Alternatively a strip of newspaper, folded over and over and passed round the plant, is handy. Since this may damage some of the spines, it is sometimes advisable to dig a little soil away at the top to expose the spineless base of the plant and hold it there.

Once the plant is out of its pot, the old soil should be picked away as much as possible, using a pointed stick, and a look-out kept for various pests (see p. 42). Be careful not to pull away too many of the fine root-hairs, to which small soil particles will cling. Dead or broken roots should be cut back to living tissue, with a razor-blade or very sharp knife. Cut surfaces are best dusted with sulphur or charcoal dust. This cutting back should be carried out even if for some reason most of the roots have died, and any decay on the plant should also be dealt with (see p. 44). Clean off dead leaves, dry skin, etc.

The new pot should accommodate the roots easily, with a little room—only a little—to spare. If the plant is large but the roots are limited, a shallow pan is desirable, or the result may be top heavy. Conversely, a plant with a long tap-root, like many cacti, needs a long narrow pot.

A large crock should cover the hole, and this be covered with two layers of small crocks. A layer of stone chips can be placed over this. There is no need to overdo the drainage: all that is necessary is to ensure that excess water which percolates through the soil should be able to run out freely, without any danger of keeping the soil wet and stagnant.

The plant should be replaced so that the soil comes up to the original level. Hold it in position and let the fresh soil trickle in round the roots, tapping the pot on the bench to shake it down, and if necessary pushing the soil in with a stick. The soil should be firm but not rammed down, and come up to about $\frac{1}{2}$ in. below the pot rim. A layer of small stone chips on the surface will prevent caking.

Before placing the soil in the pot it should be well moistened, making sure that it is damp throughout. It is no use filling a pot with dry soil—it is amazing how some particles can remain bone-dry. This slight dampness will also mean that the roots can make new absorptive hairs and take hold of the new soil readily, while soaking a freshly potted plant may cause rot. It should not be necessary to water a newly potted plant for two or three weeks.

Plants in Bowls The average fancier of succulent plants will keep his plants in separate pots, which allows full individual control of watering. He will, indeed, turn up his nose at plants kept in bowls. But for the person with only a few plants, particularly if they are kept in a living-room, bowl arrangement is both convenient and far more decorative than a number of pots.

Obviously only plants with similar requirements should be grown together. It is no use growing *Aizoaceae* with a winter growing period together with cacti which rest at that time. But the great majority of succulents can be treated alike.

It is best to use wide, shallow bowls with drainage holes, and earthenware seed-pans are ideal. If these are used, planting and culture are the same as for plants in separate pots. However, such bowls are seldom decorative, and if kept in a room need a plate below them to prevent water pouring out on to the furniture. It is perfectly possible to keep succulents in bowls without drainage, and in glazed bowls at that; I myself kept a considerable number in bowls for five years.

If this is done, it is essential to have a deep layer of small crocks, so that if surplus water collects it is well away from the soil; it is equally important to keep watering to a minimum to prevent too much water collecting, especially in winter. Even so, it is surprising how much water such bowls can receive, and how quickly it will evaporate in warm weather. The bowls are usually shallow, and the deep layer of crocks means a relatively thin layer of soil. Under such conditions the plants may not grow very fast, but obviously it is undesirable for plants in bowls to grow too large. Small plants, seedlings or cuttings, such as are sold by florists, are ideal for such bowls. Give them reasonable room, and repot every year to make sure that the roots—which will tend to spread sideways—do not get starved or tangled together.

Many of the bowls sold by florists must be regarded as temporary arrangements. The plants are almost always too large and too crowded together. They will swamp each other, and then show signs of ill-health as the roots struggle to find nourishment. Often, too, such bowl gardens contain plants requiring different treatment.

Staging As with any kind of pot plant, succulents should be placed on the staging so that they are graded in size from front to back, ensuring that they all receive enough light, that they are easily reached and that the effect is pleasing. For the latter reason also, if none other, the plants should be well spaced apart.

A small shelf at the back of the staging may be useful for display if the collection consists mostly of small plants, and also to place hanging plants on. Alternatively, such plants can be placed on an inverted pot.

Some growers bury their pots up to the rims in a deep bed of grit or gravel. This is, in fact, advisable with the small *Aizoaceae* and other tricky plants, since the bed is watered, not the pots, and the dangers of direct watering are avoided. The roots emerge from the drainage holes and seek moisture in the bed of grit. Of course, plants with different resting periods must be kept well apart.

This is admirable if one does not want to take the plants to shows, and if one has the patience to leave a semi-permanent arrangement alone. It permits a more naturalistic display, and the 'stone-imitating' plants, for instance, can be grouped with similar stones to demonstrate their camouflage. Small grit is placed over the whole surface, hiding the pot rims.

Direct planting into the soil cannot be recommended unless the arrangement is to be well-nigh permanent.

Plants Outside Some authorities recommend placing the succulents outside in the garden during the summer, when all danger of frost has passed, burying them in their pots in a well-drained bed or even planting them out. This certainly helps the plants to make strong, well-ripened growth. However, heavy rain may damage the plants or splash them with mud, while hail and unexpected early frosts are disastrous. Plants with strict growing periods may receive too much rain. Slugs and snails, too, must be kept off.

Apart from these practical considerations, few of us have vacant beds into which a collection can be moved, and the labour involved is considerable; while the effect in an English garden is at best bizarre.

Watering   Most succulent plants take as much water as any pot plant when in full growth, but since they are constructed to exist with little, it is better to under-water than to kill the roots by over-watering.

At the beginning of the growing period water is given occasionally, and gradually increased as required. As with ordinary plants, watering is only necessary when the soil begins to dry out after the previous application. The soil on the surface may look dry, but to make sure it is best to scrape down a little, or when experience is gained to judge by tapping or lifting the pot.

With almost all cacti and most of the other succulents whose growing period coincides with our summer, three or more waterings a week may be needed in hot weather. Obviously, plants in small pots, and those with vigorous root systems, will need a lot of water.

Towards the end of the growing period—about mid-September for the average succulent—watering is gradually curtailed; this helps ripening. Cacti may shrivel a little at this time, but this is quite natural. In the resting period one light watering a week is ample, and if the conditions are on the cold side, much less may suffice. In winter only enough water should be given to prevent the soil from drying out completely. At this time especially, *if in doubt do not water*: the roots are entirely inactive. Do not splash water about: this may lead to condensation on the plants if the temperature falls.

Succulents with clearly defined rest periods must *not* be watered according to the calendar. Not until the first signs of new growth are clearly visible should watering begin; and as soon as the plant begins to shrivel watering should be sharply restricted, and with many plants, as specified in the List of Genera, entirely stopped. Otherwise rotting often follows, or at least flowering may be prevented. Seedlings may, however, be watered sparingly in their first 'resting' period, with one or two exceptions. With these plants it is always best to be cautious about quantities. The method of watering grit in which pots are buried is best (see p. 29).

The best time to water plants is early in the morning or late in the afternoon, when the plants are not in hot sunshine. Never pour water on to plants; if it collects in the crown of a cactus or on top of a very succulent stone mimic, rotting will follow very rapidly. Also drops of water on a plant may act as lenses and cause ugly scorch marks in hot sun.

Some growers syringe their plants very lightly in the early evening to simulate the desert dew. This may be recommended in very hot weather, but in our climate, with air that is usually quite moist enough, it is rarely necessary and can very easily be overdone. An occasional spray, with water to which a little soft soap has been added, is useful to clean the plants, especially in the sooty, acid-laden air of towns or in dusty rooms. On such occasions the plant should be sprayed again with clear water, and then shaken to make sure no water lodges in any crevice. Woolly cacti may be 'shampooed' with a soft brush dipped in soapy water, and succulents with stiff leaves, such as Agaves and Aloes, may be gently scrubbed with a soft rag dipped in soapy water and then cleaned off with clear water.

Rainwater is best, especially in districts where there is much chlorine in the mains water. In winter and spring the chill should be taken off the water; the easiest way being to stand it for some hours in the greenhouse or room in which the plants are.

KEEPING SUCCULENTS IN ROOMS

It is quite easy to cultivate succulents in rooms, though some may fail, usually the highly adapted forms. The main requirement is sunlight, and therefore a more or less southerly aspect is best, placing the plants as near to the window as possible.

A collection of pots can be accommodated in earthenware pans, and if these are filled up with coarse sand or gravel, a generous layer being left below the pots, they will look more attractive and will not dry out too quickly. This applies particularly to the very small plants often sold by florists. Alternatively they can be planted direct into pans or bowls (see p. 27). Boxes of window-box shape can also be used.

The window-sill is the best place for them, but is often too narrow. However, a wide wooden board, supported on angle brackets, may be fixed to the sill, or if this is undesirable, legs may be fitted, either to make a removable table-like support or so that one side rests on the existing sill. Such a board may be treated just like the staging in a greenhouse and, if equipped with upright sides, may be filled up with grit.

Other possibilities are the placing of boards across window spaces or building little platforms up the sides of the window.

During the summer, air is as important as sun. At least the windows should be opened at all opportunities; if possible, the plants should be placed outside. If the window-ledge is not wide enough, some sort of board, tray or even a projecting frame with glass sides and removable lid can be fixed outside, making sure the supports are strong enough. The lid is useful in heavy rain.

With all these adjuncts, a waterproof lining, such as zinc, may be added to prevent damage to the wood and water dripping where it is not wanted.

Watering follows the rules already laid down. If the room is heated in winter, the pots will dry out rapidly and should be watered more often. But be very cautious, as over-watering in poor light conditions leads to soft growth which rots all too readily. It is really best to withdraw the plants to a room where the temperature is fairly constant and cool.

Guard against frost and draughts. Plants on window-sills may have to be removed, or protected with paper or curtains, if it is very cold outside. Do not draw curtains so as to leave plants overnight between them and the window: if it is freezing outside the plants will certainly suffer.

Plants on a window-sill or ledge should be turned periodically so that each side receives adequate sunshine.

LABELS AND RECORDS

The correct and legible naming of a plant collection will be essential to anyone who becomes sufficiently interested. There are various labels which are supplied with plants or may be bought as blanks. I much prefer the unobtrusive ivorine labels, about $\frac{5}{8}$ in. by $\frac{1}{2}$ in., with a small point below, which are inscribed with Indian ink. On elongated labels the names have to be written longwise, which means contorting oneself to read them; they are less attractive than the small square types. It is neater to have all plants with similar labels. Ivorine can be obtained in strips and cut as required.

Plants bought from florists may be wrongly labelled, either from the nurseryman's ignorance or, more usually, because the labels have fallen out in transit and been pushed back anywhere. Correction of these can only be made as experience increases, and on the basis of visits to good collections.

A written record of each plant's career, with date and place of purchase, dates of repotting, flowering, etc., will add to the interest and will help to avoid mistakes. A card index or loose-leaf book is the best method.

CHAPTER THREE

PROPAGATION

From Seed Succulents are raised from seed as easily as most tropical plants, but some grow very slowly from seedlings, especially some cacti. Seed of many species is available in Britain but may often (and probably accidentally) be hybrid.

A mixture of sterile soil, sand and peat may be used, or the John Innes seed compost is suitable. This is composed of 2 parts by bulk of sterilized loam, 1 part of peat and 1 part of coarse sand, all passed through a $\frac{1}{2}$-in. mesh sieve. Add $\frac{3}{4}$ oz. crushed chalk per bushel. This mixture is adequate if the seedlings are to be moved on quickly; if they are to remain in the same compost $1\frac{1}{2}$ oz. superphosphate per bushel should be added.

Pots, pans or seed-boxes may be used. They should be very well crocked. The seed is often very small, and if dust-like should not be covered; otherwise a very light sifting of fine sand is adequate; large seeds may be lightly pressed in. Seeds should be well spaced. The receptacle should be soaked by immersing up to the edge: top watering would disturb the seed. A sprinkling of Cheshunt compound through a very fine spray will help to avoid damping-off and the growth of algae.

These seeds need a temperature of 70° to germinate well, and a propagating frame (i.e. a small closed frame, glass-topped, with bottom heat and half filled with damp peat) is the ideal place to germinate them. If this is impossible, a warm place must be found and the receptacle covered with a sheet of glass, and preferably placed in a box containing damp peat to supply adequate moisture.

If bottom heat is available, sowing can be done in February or March; if not, wait until April or May. When germination begins air must be adequate or damping-off will occur. At this moment, too, adequate light is essential or the seedlings will be weak and spindly. Some seedlings appear after a few days; some take up to a month, and some much longer, especially if the seed is not fresh. Hence the advisability of sowing each kind in a separate receptacle. Seeds should remain viable for at least 2 years.

Quick-growing seedlings may be pricked off (i.e. replanted in other receptacles) soon after germination; but most seedlings grow so slowly at first that it is best to sow very thinly, and leave the little plants in their pans for some months, until they are at least $\frac{1}{2}$ in. in diameter or 1 in. tall, according to shape. A miniature two-pronged fork made from a piece of thin wood is useful for lifting seedlings. Care should be taken not to damage the fine roots when lifting them, and the seedlings should not be firmed too hard into the new soil.

Small seedlings should be moved into the J.I. seed compost; larger ones into the adult compost already described. Individual pots are best, but several seedlings can be placed in one pan.

Watering must be carefully attended to both before

and after germination. The boxes, pans or pots should never become quite dry. Bottom watering is best until the plants are fairly large. The resting season should not, normally, be observed until the second year, when the plants become adults.

Great care must be taken to keep away slugs, snails and woodlice, and to make sure of preventing damping-off water monthly with Cheshunt compound.

Protection from scorching sun is also necessary.

By Cuttings The majority of succulents are readily increased by cuttings. Apart from mere multiplication of specimens, it is often possible to improve the shape of a weak or a distorted plant by taking cuttings from it, for the removal of a part often promotes fresh growth; alternatively the old plant can be replaced by the better-grown youngster. But the mere pleasure of rooting new plants so easily should not allow one to spoil a well-shaped plant, particularly if it is a cactus with a number of offsets attractively growing around it. Some people think it necessary to remove such offsets; but this is not so.

The parts of a plant which can be used vary according to the family (Fig. 3). Most cacti produce young plantlets or offsets; or branches can be used. With Opuntias the pads, and with Epiphyllums the stem-segments, are used; with the latter pieces of 2 or 3 segments are advisable. Wherever a stem is jointed, not less than one joint should be used. Columnar cacti can be beheaded and the top pieces rooted; those with long thin stems are cut up into suitable lengths. Clump-forming cacti can be separated.

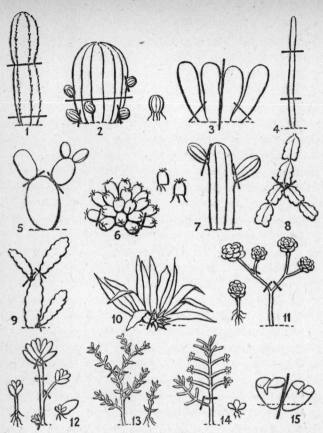

3. Propagation by cuttings and offsets: the black line shows position of cut. *1* to *4*. various cacti; *5*. *Opuntia* with pads, *6*. *Mammillaria* (tubercles); *7*. branching cactus or *Euphorbia*; *8*. *Zygocactus*; *9*. other jointed plants; *10*. offset on rosette plant; *11*. branching rosette plant, e.g. *Aeonium*; *12*. branching *Crassulaceae*; leaves can often be used; *13*. branching shrubby *Mesembryanthemum*; *14*. *Bryophyllum* (adventitious buds); *15*. *Lithops* type: divide clump or take cutting.

The tubercles of Mammillarias and similar genera can be cut off and rooted, though usually enough offsets are produced.

Cactus-like succulents, such as many Euphorbias and *Stapelia* and its relations, are treated in the same way, separating branches or offsets or beheading columnar stems. The latter method obviously ruins the parent plant, and is usually only resorted to when the base is damaged or has become woody.

Agaves, Aloes, Haworthias, Gasterias, etc., produce easily removed offsets. Many kinds of *Bryophyllum* and *Kalanchoë* produce adventitious buds on the leaves, which make roots while still on the parent. Almost all succulents can be increased by stem cuttings, and most *Crassulaceae* by leaves as well. The leaves are usually very easily detached, and if pushed into sandy compost root and produce new leaves around the base. They will even produce roots if left lying on a damp soil surface. Leaves of *Aloe* and *Haworthia* will also root.

The *Aizoaceae* can be increased by stem cuttings; leaves will not root. The shrubby species root readily, but the fleshy ones are more difficult. Each pair of leaves, or plant-body in the highly succulent forms, can be treated as a cutting; the base of the plant must be undamaged.

Cuttings can be taken at any time, but late spring and high summer are best. At other times there is the danger of rotting due to damp and cold. Bottom heat is helpful but not essential. If the pots or boxes can be watered from the bottom so much the better—a thin layer of damp peat will help this; but avoid a close atmosphere, which may provoke basal decay. Shade from full sun is advisable.

For rooting, the usual potting compost, with some extra grit, can be used, but pure coarse silver sand, or a mixture of sand and peat, is better; vermiculite, which holds moisture like the peat mixture, promotes very quick rooting. With all these the plants need to be potted up fairly soon after rooting, as no food is present. Perhaps the best method is to place the cuttings in a layer of coarse sand or vermiculite over the potting mixture.

The most important thing when taking cuttings of these plants is to dry them well. After making the cut, with a sharp knife or razor-blade, the cuttings must be left in a warm, dry place until a *callus*, or skin, has formed over the cut surface. With very fleshy cacti or Mesembryanthemums, a period of several weeks may be needed. Never insert a cutting until the cut is well and truly dried, nor over-water the rooting material. The pieces to be rooted need not be pushed in at all deeply.

Grafting   Most cacti can be grafted on to other cacti. I have never heard of grafting practised on other kinds of succulent, but it is presumably feasible in some instances.

There are occasions when grafting helps a weakly or slow-growing cactus to grow more strongly, or quickly, or allows the cultivation of species which are almost impossible to grow on their own roots. Sometimes a hanging cactus is grafted to the top of a columnar form to produce a result like a weeping standard rose. Apart from these more or less necessary cases, I think grafted plants are ugly and unnecessary, though sometimes grotesque combinations may elicit a reluctant fascination.

The basis of cactus grafting is to make flat cuts which correspond on stock and scion, and to press them together immediately. Horizontal, V or Λ-shaped cuts may be used. When the scion is a thin or flattened plant, such as *Aporocactus* or *Zygocactus* respectively, a wedge graft is used; a narrow cleft should be cut in the stock, and the edges of the scion should be pared of the outer skin to provide sufficient cut surface.

Zygocactus is sometimes grafted fanwise on to large *Opuntia* pads. Very thin round stems, such as of *Pereskia*, may be pushed into a hole in a large cactus. All sorts of combinations will suggest themselves.

The two parts are generally pinned together, usually with an unbarbed cactus spine, which will not rust like a metal pin. Alternatively, rubber bands or string are placed around the base of the pot and the graft, using paper or cotton-wool as padding if necessary.

Union should occur in a week or two. If the plants are pinned together, the spine should be removed after about a week, to avoid rotting; but other fixing should be left for three weeks. In any case, great care should be taken to avoid jolting the union during the first three weeks. Nor should any water reach the point of union during this time, or rotting may occur. Otherwise conditions are the same as for normal plants.

Grafting should be done in summer when the day temperature is between 65° and 70°, and when the atmosphere is dry. Full ventilation should be given to promote air circulation.

CHAPTER FOUR

PESTS AND DISEASES

PESTS

SUCCULENTS are attacked by the same pests as most greenhouse plants, but these are quite easily dealt with provided excessive infestation is not allowed to occur. Routine individual examination and treatment are best, and all-over spraying or fumigation should only be a last resort.

Ants These may disturb and damage roots, and sometimes introduce greenfly. *Control:* The best thing is to find the nest and destroy it with boiling water or by pouring in carbon disulphide, or at least find and block their entry into the greenhouse. Otherwise use a proprietary ant-killer, or BHC or DDT dust.

Aphides The ordinary greenfly may attack succulents. *Control:* Spray with BHC, HETP or nicotine emulsion.

Mealy Bug This is the commonest pest. A relation of the aphis, it is white, woolly and about $\frac{1}{8}$ in. long. *Control:* Pick off individual insects with a paint-brush dipped in soapy water. Spray with HETP, nicotine emulsion or 20 per cent wettable DDT, using 1 teaspoonful of the latter to a quart of water. Fumigate with nicotine or DDT fumigant.

Red Spider If plants have white or yellow markings, a webbed appearance, or begin to shrivel, red spider should be suspected (but see also Starvation, p. 45). These tiny

red mites can only be seen under a lens. *Control:* Spray
with derris or HETP, or fumigate with Azobenzene.

Root Mealy Bug Similar to mealy bug, but infests
roots, making white woolly patches. If the plant looks
unhealthy, look at the roots. *Control:* The soil must be
shaken off and the pests removed as much as possible.
The roots should then be dipped into soapy water with
2 per cent pure nicotine added, and allowed to dry before
repotting. As a deterrent, the plants may be watered with
a nicotine solution, 1 teaspoonful per quart of water, or
with a prepared nicotine emulsion, or a few crystals of
paradichlorbenzene or flakes of naphthalene may be
placed among the crocks.

Scale Insects Small waxy mounds about $\frac{3}{32}$ in. across
are the covering of scale insects, a kind of aphis that
settles down in one place. *Control:* Spraying with nicotine or HETP is fairly effective; it is best to use a paint-
brush soaked in the insecticidal solution to remove the
scale bodily, or to move each scale with a blunt stick.

Slugs and Snails Considerable damage can be done by
these creatures, and regular inspection should be made.
Control: Proprietary meta-and-bran baits.

Thrips Small grey or white marks on plants may be
caused by these insects, which are very thin, about $\frac{1}{8}$ in.
long, and jump. *Control:* Spray with BHC or DDT.

Woodlice These pests may attack plants, especially
seedlings. *Control:* Use DDT dust, a poison bait ($1\frac{1}{2}$ lb.
bran or dried blood, 1 oz. Paris Green), or attract the
pests with a scooped-out turnip or potato.

Note: Nicotine and HETP are poisons. Do not get

them on the skin nor breathe the spray. Follow maker's instructions at all times, especially when fumigating. Do not spray in full sunlight; early in the day is best.

DISEASES

The diseases of succulents are perhaps more difficult to deal with, because their main cause is faulty cultivation.

Damping-off Seedlings of succulents may suffer from damping-off, when they rot at the base and fall over. Care in watering, adequate ventilation and sterile compost will help to avert this; as an additional precaution, Chinosol or Cheshunt compound (standard remedies) should be used on the seed-pans—say every month.

Dry Rot This is a mysterious disease, in which the plants shrivel and parts become dry and withered. Even if such parts are removed, the rest of the plant usually dies. It is commonest in the resting period, and the only thing to do is to try to force the plant into growth, *slowly*, with extra warmth and watering.

Frost Frost damage is superficially similar to soft rot, though in bad cases the result is a slimy mass and the plant is finished. Slightly frosted plants should be thawed out slowly, any damaged part removed, and dusted as suggested for soft rot.

Mildew There is a kind of mildew which attacks cacti, producing the usual greyish film on the surface. It occurs in over-damp, airless conditions; the plant can be cleaned up with Thiram or a colloidal copper spray.

Soft Rot Rotting, usually at the base, may be due to various causes. The most common is over-watering, especially if associated with a heavy soil or bad drainage. Rotting at the top of a plant is most often due to water lodging there. Rot may also follow soft growth caused by over-feeding, or by fermenting material in the soil such as partly decayed manure. Excessive salt in the soil or an excess of any single chemical may have the same effect. Some plants dislike full sun and may be scorched on a cloudless day; such scorch may become a seat of rot. Scorch may also follow careless watering, which leaves drops on the plant that act as burning glasses. Careless removal of cuttings or offsets may result in rot.

All these sorts of decay, which involve a fungus infection of unhealthy tissue, must be checked by removal of the infected area. In a cactus the flesh is often streaky round the soft area; these streaks must be cut right out. Sometimes the damaged area can be treated by dusting with powdered charcoal or flowers of sulphur; usually the plant is so much mutilated that only a healthy upper part is left. Fortunately most succulents root readily as cuttings, and this is the thing to do with such upper parts (see p. 37). If the root is unaffected, it should be dusted and may sprout afresh.

Starvation   When a plant has been in a pot too long the soil becomes replaced with roots. Starvation and drying out result, and the plant may begin to wither, go yellow and finally rot. Turn the plant out, remove the dead roots, cut back the top to healthy tissue and repot.

Infrequent repotting and the starvation which results are probably the most usual causes of bad health among succulents, especially cacti.

CHAPTER FIVE

THE FAMILIES OF SUCCULENTS

WHEN referring to succulents many people speak rather of 'cacti' and include in that name the other groups—if, indeed, they realize that there *are* other groups. Now, the cacti are members of the family *Cactaceae*; it is certainly an important one, but it is only one.

It is, of course, the flowers that reveal the family, the flower being the only part of the plant which retains its basic structure whatever adaptations the leaves and stems may have made. There are members of other families which are almost indistinguishable from cacti to the casual eye, but the flowers are entirely different.

The *Cactaceae* are almost exclusively natives of America. There are a few other succulents in America, but on the whole the other groups are African. The close resemblance of some American and some African species is a nice example of what science calls parallel evolution —the modification of members of unrelated families into similar forms and structures to meet a similar set of climatic conditions.

There is a certain amount of confusion among the genera. In the most important families, the *Cactaceae* and *Aizoaceae*, the first plants of each to be found were given the names, respectively, of *Cactus* and *Mesembryanthemum*. As more and more different plants were discovered, however, it soon became plain that these names were insufficient to classify the families. For it must be remembered that names are not given merely for identification; if that were so all the *Cactaceae* might, indeed, be regarded as different species of a genus *Cactus*. But names are also a guide to classification, and similar species are grouped into single genera.

Thus the families have been gradually divided into more and more genera as the botanists find details which will segregate them, and botanists differ in their ideas of what generic and specific names also may be accepted. This accounts for the various names under which some plants may be found. I have attempted to keep synonyms mentioned to the minimum, but these facts should be remembered if you see a familiar plant under another name.

In the following pages are outlined the main characteristics of the families with succulent members which are included in this book.

The Cactaceae   A family almost entirely succulent and usually leafless. The more primitive and unadapted members are those which are least succulent and may have leaves. In some, tiny growths are formed at the growing points; these are abortive leaves, which soon fall.

The cushion-like areoles are unique to the cacti. These may be covered in wool or hair, or small bristles called glochids, and may sprout spines. It is at the areoles that the flowers appear. These have a large, indeterminate number of petals and stamens; there is usually no clear distinction between petals and sepals. The ovary is 'inferior', i.e. below every other part of the flower. The flowers are usually large, showy and bright. The fruit is a single-celled berry, usually fleshy but sometimes dry, quite large and brightly coloured, with many seeds.

The cactus does not have the structure of a woody plant, but in the larger forms the vessels that conduct water from the roots form a woody skeleton, without which of course the tree-like species, which may reach 60 ft., could never stand up.

The *Cactaceae* are divided into three tribes, the *Pereskieae*, *Opuntieae* and *Cereeae*. These are described briefly below.

The Pereskieae A small group of primitive cacti which are hardly succulent at all, though the flowers confirm that they are members of the family. They are mainly twiggy bushes or sub-shrubs, bearing spines, and glossy leaves not unlike those of a camellia. The main genus is *Pereskia,* and most of the species are Mexican.

The Opuntieae An extensive tribe containing the well-known Prickly Pears. Botanically they are separated from other cacti by the presence of glochids in the areoles—fine, barbed bristles which can be very irritating if they enter the skin. Some have awl-shaped leaves which are often only carried for a short time, and the stems are divided into more or less regular joints which are usually flattened. The main genus, *Opuntia,* contains many species and is much subdivided by botanists. There are 7 or 8 other genera. The *Opuntia* tribe spreads from Canada to Cape Horn, and has been naturalized in the Mediterranean area, Australia and elsewhere.

The Cereeae This tribe contains the majority of cacti,

THE FAMILIES OF SUCCULENTS

and its members are found from Canada to Patagonia. Owing to its size, it is naturally much subdivided; the various groups are given below.

Group 1. With ribs, angles or tubercles; usually spiny.

Sub-tribe *Cereaneae*. Usually much branched, often making bushes or tree-like. Around 40 genera. Most important: *Borzicactus, Cephalocereus, Cereus, Cleistocactus, Lemaireocereus, Trichocereus*.

Sub-tribe *Hylocereaneae*. Climbing plants with aerial roots. About 9 genera. Most important: *Aporocactus, Hylocereus* and *Selenicereus*.

Sub-tribe *Echinocereaneae*. Short-stemmed, clump-forming, flowering from the lateral areoles. 6 or 7 genera. Most important: *Echinocereus, Echinopsis, Lobivia* and *Rebutia*.

Sub-tribe *Echinocactaneae*. Similar to the last but flowering from areoles near the growing point of the stem. At least 33 genera. Most important: *Ferocactus, Gymnocalycium, Notocactus* and *Parodia*.

Sub-tribe *Cactanae*. Usually globular. With two kinds of areole, one bearing spines, on the stem, and the other from which the flowers appear, at the top. Includes the original genus *Cactus*, or *Melocactus*, very difficult to grow.

Sub-tribe *Coryphanthanae*. Globular and tubercled, with two kinds of areole, one bearing spines, at the tips of tubercles, and the other, often wool-bearing, from which flowers appear, on the sides or at the base of tubercles. About 14 genera. Most important: *Mammillaria* and *Coryphantha.*

Group 2. Epiphytic plants with usually flattened stems, usually spineless.

Sub-tribe *Epiphyllanae.* Stems flattened; flowers with tube. 9 genera. Most important: *Epiphyllum.*

Sub-tribe *Rhipsalidanae.* Stems variable, flattened or rounded, with ribs; flowers with no tube. 8 genera. Most important: *Rhipsalis.*

The Aizoaceae This is a family (sometimes called *Ficoidaceae* or *Mesembryanthemaceae*) exclusively composed of succulents, from S. and S.W. Africa. The species used to be classed under the single genus *Mesembryanthemum,* but this has been greatly divided up, and the name now only refers to a few shrubby species. Some confusion of naming still exists.

The flowers of the *Aizoaceae* are bi-sexual, with either many petals or none, 4 or 5 sepals, 4, 5 or many stamens, and an ovary of 2 or more cells giving rise to a capsular fruit. Many are large and bright in a wide range of colours, and superficially resemble daisies.

They exhibit gradations of form according to the amount of specialization imposed by the habitat. First there are shrubby, more or less woody plants, with leaves arranged in well-spaced opposite pairs, one pair at right angles to the next. These are usually easy to grow, flower freely and are often used for bedding out. These include *Carpobrotus, Delosperma, Drosanthemum, Lampranthus, Ruschia,* the few remaining species of *Mesembryanthemum,* and at least 16 other genera (Fig. 4).

4. Some shrubby plants of the *Mesembryanthemum* group. 1. *Lampranthus roseus*; 2. *Oscularia deltoides*; 3. *Delosperma echinatum*; 4. *Carpobrotus edulis*.

Then there are plants with fairly long stems but much fleshier leaves, more closely packed on the stems. These merge into the really fleshy forms, where the stems are almost or entirely absent, often with only a few pairs of leaves, still in the cruciate pattern which is, in such forms, much more marked, though sometimes obscured by crowding. The most important among these, out of about 45 genera, are *Argyroderma, Bergeranthus, Cheiridopsis, Faucaria, Gibbaeum, Glottiphyllum, Nananthus, Pleiospilos, Stomatium* and *Titanopsis* (Figs. 5 and 17).

The next stage comes when these leaves are reduced to two; there are forms in which the leaves are partly joined, and these lead into those in which the leaves have been converted into a single solid mass or plant-body. The division between the pair is sometimes marked by a groove or slit, may be reduced to a small aperture or may

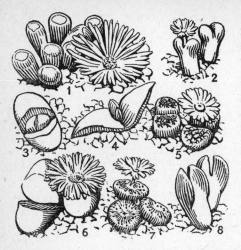

5. Some of the most highly adapted *Aizoaceae*. 1. *Fenestraria aurantiaca*; 2. *Ophthalmophyllum Friedrichiae*; 3. *Gibbaeum dispar*; 4. *G. velutinum*; 5. *Lithops Julii*; 6. *Argyroderma octophyllum*; 7. *Conophytum Nevillei*; 8. *C. bilobum*.

have disappeared. This is a smaller group of about 8 genera, notably *Conophytum*, *Lithops* and *Ophthalmophyllum* (Fig. 5).

These are most surprising when they produce their flowers, which are often bigger than the bodies themselves. At other times many of these succulents are very difficult to see, since their shape and colouring are so similar to the surrounding stones. They have therefore been nicknamed 'living stones' or 'stone mimics'. This is an example of natural selection; those plants which showed up too clearly were eaten by birds and browsing animals, those which were camouflaged continued to multiply. Thus, as the character of the stones in the deserts alters so do the species to be found.

Apart from these are two 'window plants' (see p. 12),

Fenestraria and *Frithia,* which might be taken for plant bodies, but which are, in fact, groups of cylindrical leaves arising from one stem.

Then there is a very curious group including *Conophyllum, Mitrophyllum* and *Monilaria,* which produce two different kinds of leaves and are of peculiar shape (Fig. 15).

Lastly there is a group of annuals, small branching plants, two of which, *Cryophytum* and *Dorotheanthus,* are commonly treated as half-hardy annuals and can be very showy.

The Crassulaceae This next-largest family of succulent plants includes many hardy species. The leaves are usually either in opposite pairs at right angles, in rosettes or arranged spirally up the stem. The flowers, usually carried in a cluster, are bi-sexual and regular, with 4 or 5 petals and sepals.

The names of the genera have been very much muddled, and one species may have three or four generic synonyms. One group is centred on the hardy *Sempervivum,* and includes the tender *Aeonium* and *Greenovia. Sedum,* the Stonecrop, is another genus which is fairly clearly defined.

The other important genera are *Adromischus, Bryophyllum, Cotyledon, Crassula, Echeveria, Kalanchoë, Pachyphytum, Rochea.*

Many of these are very attractive, and almost all are easy to grow, apart from some very specialized desert Crassulas. They are widely distributed in America, Africa and to a lesser extent Asia, and show succulent forms provoked not only by heat and drought but by cold and drought (see p. 10).

The Asclepiadaceae   This family is far from exclusively succulent. The succulent genera are on the whole African, though widely scattered in that continent, and there are some from India and the East Indies. Most of them are leafless and superficially cactus-like, the genus *Stapelia* being the type. The family has been expanded into other genera as more species were discovered, and in the process some confusion has been created.

The *Asclepiadaceae* have bizarre flowers, reaching the height of oddity in *Ceropegia*. Botanically they are regular; the anthers are joined to the stigma; and the seeds, which are produced in a pair of long horn-like follicles, are usually tufted with hair, a dispersal device.

The Compositae   It would be surprising if the largest of all plant families had not produced some succulent forms. The huge genus *Senecio*, which includes our native Ragwort and Groundsel, contains a number of diverse succulent forms exhibiting different stages of adaptation to drought. The related *Kleinia* contains species equally diverse in form. All have typical composite flowers, disconcertingly like those of Groundsel. Most of the species come from South and South-west Africa; others from other parts of Africa and from the East Indies.

The Euphorbiaceae   One of the most extensive single genera, *Euphorbia* contains a large number of succulent forms, mostly very cactus-like, but distinguishable partly by the entirely dissimilar flowers and by usually having

54

milky juice. The genus displays the most astonishing diversity of form and adaptation. The flowers are of two sexes, usually carried in cyathia, in which a petalless female flower is surrounded by brighter petal-like structures. Sometimes the male and female flowers are carried on separate plants. Very often leaves are absent or primitive.

The succulent Euphorbias occur in South and North Africa, Madagascar, Canary Islands, Arabia, E. Indies, a few in America, and are naturalized elsewhere.

The Liliaceae The succulent *Liliaceae* are mainly rosette plants, the leaves being often, as in *Aloe*—one of the most widely spread African succulents—held at the end of a woody stem. Other genera are *Apicra, Gasteria* (in which the leaves are carried in two rows) and *Haworthia* (which includes several 'window plants'). *Schizobasopsis,* better known as *Boweia,* and one species of *Scilla* (*S. violacea*) form overground bulbs.

The flowers of these plants are like trumpet lilies in miniature, carried on long stems, but often insignificant and rarely showy.

Less Important Families Among the 17 other families which have a few succulent species, the following are mentioned in this book. Representatives of the families not described are either rare in nature, or in commerce, or very difficult to cultivate.

Amaryllidaceae The Amaryllis family is represented by the extensive American genus *Agave*. This is also naturalized in Europe and Africa.

Geraniaceae The common Pelargoniums so much used

for bedding in this country are themselves more or less fleshy; and there are several really succulent members of this genus from arid regions of South and South-west Africa, as well as the entirely leafless, greatly drought-resisting *Sarcocaulon* (rarely grown), from the same area.

Portulacaceae This family, represented in Britain by Purslane and other weedy plants, is naturally fleshy, and it is difficult to draw the line as to which are succulents and which are not, but the following very different forms are usually accepted as such. One species, the Brazilian *Portulaca grandiflora*, is familiar as the parent of a race of showy half-hardy annuals. Then there is *Portulacaria afra*, from South Africa, almost identical in appearance to a Crassula; and the fairly large genus *Anacampseros* from South and South-west Africa, and including one Australian species, which either makes fleshy rosettes or highly drought-adapted forms with tiny leaves and scaly protective covering.

Vitaceae The vine family is represented by a number of African species of *Cissus*, a genus mostly of climbers, with greatly swollen stems from which, in the growing season, large fleshy leaves are produced.

CHAPTER SIX

LIST OF GENERA

IN the list that follows I have briefly described 81 genera and their culture, mainly those which are relatively easy to grow and obtain, but including a few which are not but are too important or remarkable in some way to pass over. Both to save space and to lessen confusion, no synonyms have been mentioned except where really necessary. The following abbreviations are used:

Min.: Minimum.　　　　T.: Temperature.
Max.: Maximum.　　　　R.: Resting period.
P.: Method of propagation.　W.: Winter.

The resting period may vary from species to species, and is only a generalization; cultivation should never rely on the calendar (see p. 31). Where no resting period is indicated or specific details about watering or temperature are not given, the average treatment described in Chapter Two should be followed. Since with few exceptions all cacti can be readily increased from both seeds and cuttings, and offsets where produced, no specific details of propagation are given for these. Temperatures are quoted in degrees Fahrenheit.

Adromischus (*Crassulaceae*) Low-growing plants, sometimes with short stems, and leaves varying from flat and spoon-shaped to fat and club-shaped or rounded; often nicely mottled, from $\frac{1}{2}$ in. to 4 in. long. Flowers small, in spikes or clusters, pink or white. All are worth growing. Min. W.T., 50°. P., seed, stem cuttings or leaves.

Aeonium (*Crassulaceae*)   Attractive plants making tight rosettes, similar to the hardy *Sempervivum,* but tender and often with long branching stems. The leaves, sometimes toothed or edged with hairs, are less fleshy, and the rosettes are open, bowl-shaped or, as in *A. tabulaeforme* (Fig. 1), quite flat. The small bright flowers, red, pink, white or yellow, are packed into much-branched clusters, often produced only after several years. The rosettes that produce flowers die afterwards. Some (e.g. *A. canariense, A. nobile*) make large rosettes up to 2 ft. across, and correspondingly large flower-heads. Others (e.g. *A. domesticum*) make nice little miniature trees.

Easy and worth-while to grow, and thrive in rooms. In winter only frost protection is needed. Max. W.T., 50°. P., seed, very quick from cuttings.

Agave (*Amaryllidaceae*) (Fig. 1)   Rosette plants, usually with very hard leaves with spines along the edges, often variegated with white, yellow, pink or pale green. The leaves are usually broadly lanceolate but sometimes very narrow. A trunk is sometimes formed. Some eventually grow to great size. Flowers on upright spikes, often only appearing after many years; individual rosettes die after flowering. Most make attractive pot plants when small. Easy to grow, most needing only frost protection, and resist neglect; useful in tubs in the summer. P., seed, offsets.

Aloe (*Liliaceae*)   Rather dull plants, usually forming rosettes, or sometimes with leaves in two rows, and often with long stems. Rosettes similar to Agaves, but leaves usually fewer, often toothed. Flowers, sometimes showy, red, orange or yellow, on long stalks. Commonly cultivated is *A. variegata,* the 'partridge aloe' (Fig. 1), with stubby dark green leaves with many white marks. *A. aristata* makes a hemispherical rosette with narrow leaves edged and covered with white teeth. Tough, easy plants, good in rooms; frost protection only; plenty of water in summer. P., seed, offsets, sometimes from leaf cuttings. Repot in late summer.

Apicra (*Liliaceae*) Small tough plants, useful although dull, with long ascending rosettes, sometimes spirally twisted, usually with thorny tubercles. Related to *Haworthia*: culture the same; easy in rooms.

Aporocactus (*Cactaceae*) The 'rat's-tail cacti', epiphytes with long, trailing, ribbed stems up to 3 ft. or more, around $\frac{1}{2}$ in. thick, covered with small spines. Needs growing in a basket or does well when grafted on a columnar cactus such as *Nyctocereus serpentinus* or *Selenicereus spp.* The pink or red flowers, about 3 in. long, appear in late spring. Best known and very widely grown—a favourite cottage window plant—is *A. flagelliformis*. Prefers a rich, peaty, lime-free soil, with cow manure and plenty of root space. Wet and warm in the growing season. Min. W.T., 50°–55°.

Argyroderma (*Aizoaceae*) (Fig. 5) Small stemless plants, usually making only one or two pairs of thick leaves, each pair joined at the base; often forming clumps. The leaves are usually rounded outside and flat on the inner faces of the pair, but are sometimes fingerlike (e.g. *A. Braunsii*). Flower freely, in various colours. *A. roseum* has flowers over 3 in. across. Min. T., 50°. R., mainly W., varies with species; all but dry. P., seed.

Astrophytum (*Cactaceae*) The 'Star Cacti' (Fig. 6). Globular, with four to eight ribs, usually well marked, spineless in *A. Asterias* and *A. myriostigma*, with stiff spines in *A. ornatum* and papery spines in *A. capricorne*.

6. A group of Astrophytums or Star Cacti. 1. *A. capricorne nivea*; 2. *A. ornatum*; 3. *A. Asterias*; 4. *A. myriostigma*.

The four-ribbed *A. myriostigma quadricostata* is sometimes called 'Parson's Cap'. The bodies are covered with tiny white tufts. The flowers are large and yellow. Water with care. Easily grown and very attractive.

Bergeranthus (*Aizoaceae*) Stemless, making rosettes of up to 8 narrow, pointed leaves, 1–5 in. long, of triangular section. Free-flowering. Max. W.T., 55°. R., W.: fairly dry. P., seed or cuttings.

60

Bryophyllum (*Crassulaceae*) Related to *Kalanchoë*. Tall, bushy plants, often shrubby in nature, making plantlets in the leaf-notches or, in *B. proliferum*, among the flowers, which are quite large, in clusters, appearing usually in autumn or winter. *B. crenatum* has oval leaves and red flowers; *B. Daigremontianum* has long triangular leaves and yellow or pink flowers; *B. tubiflorum* has

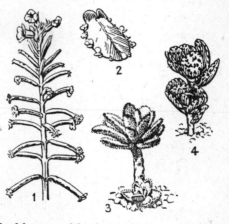

7. The Bryophyllums and Kalanchoës are closely related. 1. *B. tubiflorum*; 2. leaf of *B. crenatum*; 3. *K. tomentosa*; 4. *K. marmorata*.

long, thin, cylindrical leaves with plantlets at the end, and orange flowers (Fig. 7). They make nice room plants, needing rich soil and only slight heat in winter. P., seeds or plantlets; the latter will drop and root anywhere!

Carnegiea (*Cactaceae*) *C. gigantea*, the only species, is seldom cultivated, but deserves mention. It is the giant Sahuaro or tree-cactus of Arizona, which may attain 60 ft. in height and 2 ft. diameter. It is often branched, giving a candelabrum effect. The white flowers are about

4 in. long and wide. Very slow-growing—seedlings may make an inch a year!

Carpobrotus (*Aizoaceae*)   *C. edulis,* the 'Hottentot Fig' (Fig. 4), with its large white, magenta or yellow flowers and long, thick, triangular leaves, is a plant often seen naturalized on our south and south-west coasts. Other species are similar: *C. acinaciformis* has the largest flowers of the family, nearly 5 in. across and bright red-purple. Strong-growing plants, almost hardy, suitable for planting out in frost-free places; not so satisfactory, and shy-flowering, in pots. Very rich soil. P., cuttings best.

Cephalocereus (*Cactaceae*) Large columnar cacti, usually woolly or hairy, especially at the top, and with spines. The wool and spines only develop well on old plants. The flowers are small. Though there are scores of species, the only one commonly grown is *C. senilis,* the 'Old Man', covered with long white hairs. Rather tricky; water sparingly. Add extra limestone to the compost. Min. W.T., 50°.

Cereus (*Cactaceae*) One of the original large genera, now reduced to about 30 species, which are large, with ribbed or angular spines, columnar stems, often bluish. The flowers are large and open at night. Many of the specimens in commerce are hybrids. The most commonly seen species include steely-blue *C. chalybaeus,* with red and white flowers 7 or 8 in. long; *C. Jamacaru,* bluish-green, with even larger whitish flowers; and *C. peruvianus,* which has several cristate forms (Fig. 2). Good stock for grafting. They are all easily grown.

Ceropegia (*Asclepiadaceae*) Odd plants, either fleshy,

upright and leafless, or twiners, usually with opposite leaves. Roots often tuberous. Flowers 5-lobed, the lobes usually joined to each other at the tips; some are very curious. In *C. Haygarthii* the red and purple flower expands into a funnel, divides into lobes which bend back together into a short tube, then spread out and come together again. In *C. Sandersonii* (Fig. 18) the lobes suggest an arrangement like a fringed green umbrella. Easy to grow, even in rooms; climbers best in hanging baskets. Soil rich, with extra humus. Max. W.T., 55°. P., seeds, cuttings or aerial tubers if formed.

Chamaecereus (*Cactaceae*)   The only species, *C. Sylvestrii*, is very commonly grown. It is small, making a clump of branching, more or less prostrate pale green stems up to 6 in. long and 1 in. thick, with small white spines. In spring the scarlet flowers, about $2\frac{1}{2}$ in. long and $1\frac{1}{2}$ in. across, are profusely produced. There are cristate forms and a yellow-coloured form. Nearly hardy, and best kept between 33°–40° in winter. Easy for rooms.

Cheiridopsis (*Aizoaceae*) (Fig. 15)   An interesting genus with many very fleshy species of varying shape. 1 to 3 pairs of leaves, each pair different. Some species make longish, triangular leaves; others have a boat-shaped pair of basal leaves and short rounded central pair; others are small and rounded. Quite difficult, needing moderate watering only in the growing period, but worth specialized study. R., early spring to late summer, quite dry. Min. W.T., 45°. P., seed.

Cissus (*Vitaceae*)   Most Cissus are shrubby climbers related to the grape, and there are some succulent climbers (e.g. *C. cactiformis, C. quadrangularis*) with four-angled, ribbed, jointed stems, with leaves and tendrils at lobes and ends, which are quite easy to grow in a cool house. P., cuttings.

The really succulent species, however, are rare, peculiar and difficult. Examples are *C. Bainesii, C. Cramerianum, C. Juttae*. For much of the year, when they should be kept quite dry, they exist as conical or barrel-shaped stems with whitish, peeling skin, from 2 to 12 ft. high in nature but rarely over 1 ft. in cultivation. In winter, when they should be lightly watered, they produce large, toothed, glossy leaves in a tuft, and sometimes a spray of tiny flowers followed by berries. Maximum soil; soil poor, very porous. Min. T., 50°. P., seed.

Cleistocactus (*Cactaceae*) Columnar or sometimes prostrate, many-ribbed, up to 6 ft. tall but only 1 or 2 in. thick. The flowers are narrow and tubular, about 2 in. long. *C. Strausii* is a beautiful plant covered with small white bristles, and has red flowers. *C. nivosus* is similar, but appears white due to white hairs. *C. Baumannii* has brownish spikes and orange-red flowers. *C. smaragdiflorus* resembles it but has green tips to the red petals—a striking sight. These like a rich, leafy soil, and will stand 15° of frost if dry at the roots.

Conophyllum (*Aizoaceae*) Originally synonymous with *Mitrophyllum* (*q.v.*) and very similar, with a very brief growing period.

Conophytum (*Aizoaceae*) (Fig. 5) One of the largest and most drought-adapted genera in the family, entirely composed of small plant-bodies, the basic pair of leaves being almost entirely merged. A few form stems when aged, and these make tap-roots. Most make clumps at ground level. The bodies are round, conical, cylindrical or ovate; some have no division; some a tiny slit in the top; others have more or less pronounced lobes. The flowers emerge from the centre of the top and are $\frac{1}{2}$ to $1\frac{1}{4}$ in. across. They are easy to grow, will flower in rooms and can be increased rapidly. Min. W.T., 45°. R. September/October–July, when the outer skin becomes very withered; keep almost dry September–December; quite dry January–June/July. P., seed, division.

Coryphantha (*Cactaceae*) A large genus of low cylindrical or globular plants with more or less pronounced tubercles, resembling *Mammillaria*, but separated because of a groove on the upper surface of the tubercles. The flowers are often large, usually yellow. *C. elephantidens* has 4-in. pink flowers. *C. radians* has relatively long spines. Prefers a leafy compost. Easy to grow.

Cotyledon (*Crassulaceae*) A confused genus close to many other members of the family, containing various types of plant. Most are attractive, easy and good indoors, with a max. W.T. of 50°. These include species such as *C. macrantha, orbiculata* and *undulata,* which resemble the shrubby Crassulas. Another group, including *C. cacalioides* and *reticulata,* resemble miniature palms, with clumps of thin cylindrical leaves at the ends of long stems. These are more fussy, with a min. W.T. of 50°, and needing to be kept fully dry in the summer rest period. There are various other forms, mostly low-growing. The amateur is usually mainly interested in the first three mentioned. The flowers are carried in tall clusters, often quite attractive. P., seed, quickly from cuttings, less easily from leaves.

Crassula (*Crassulaceae*) (Fig. 8) A large genus of attractive plants of various forms, most worth cultivation. Leaves almost always opposite, often in cruciform ar-

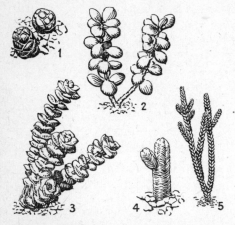

8. A few of the very variable Crassulas. 1. *C. teres*; 2. *C. argentea*; 3. *C. rupestris*; 4. *C. pyramidalis*; 5. *C. lycopodioides.*

rangement, but may be spread out on long stems or tightly packed together. The small flowers in clusters are pink, white, rarely yellow. Typical of the shrubby species are *C. arborescens, argentea* and *lactea,* stout plants with fleshy, roughly spoon-shaped leaves. In *C. perfoliata* the greyish, lanceolate leaves are closely packed in alternate pairs. *C. falcata* is similar, with rhomboidal, crosswise upright leaves, the whole plant being flattened in one vertical plane. It has large clusters of carmine flowers.

Some are trailers, attractive in baskets, such as *C.*

rupestris, corallina and *spathulata* in which small leaves, joined together at the base, are strung like beads on long stems.

In *C. lycopodioides* the tiny leaves are packed into erect, square stems up to 2 ft. high and ¼ in. thick. This is similar in structure to the 'mimicry' forms, such as *C. pyramidalis, C. columnaris, C. quadrangularis, C. arta, C. teres*; in these the stem is square or rounded, and the leaves are so close that a nearly smooth surface results.

Lastly there is a group of low-growing, very succulent forms, including *C. cornuta, C. tabularis, C. tecta.*

Most of the species are easy to grow and do well in rooms, with a max. W.T. of 50°. The 'mimicry' forms are for the expert, and should be kept to the greenhouse, needing a min. W.T. of 50°, and to be rested, nearly dry, in our summer. The last-mentioned, fleshy forms need similar conditions and rest in our winter. P., seed, readily by cuttings, also from leaves.

Cryophytum (*Aizoaceae*) *C. crystallinum*, usually sold as *Mesembryanthemum crystallinum* or Ice-plant, is an annual grown for the sparkle of its spoon-shaped leaves, caused by a protective layer of crystalline papillae. It has small white flowers. Treat like *Dorotheanthus.*

Delosperma (*Aizoaceae*) Most are small shrubs with smallish leaves, often covered with raised dots and hairs, giving a silvery, sparkling look. Commonest is *D. echinatum* (Fig. 4), whose leaves, about ½ in. long, are an elongated egg-shape. In some, as *D. Brunnthaleri,* the leaves are lanceolate. They flower freely and for many months, with small whitish or reddish blooms. Max. W.T., 50°. P., seeds, cuttings.

Dorotheanthus (*Aizoaceae*) The Livingstone Daisy, a delightful and showy little annual. Seedsmen sell it as *Mesembryanthemum criniflorum,* but the packet usually contains hybrids which produce flowers white, buff, pink or carmine, sometimes banded in two colours, about $1\frac{1}{2}$ in. across. These are superior to the species *D. criniflorus* and *D. gramineus,* and varieties of the latter. They are classed as half-hardy annuals, but are quite tough and may be sown in cold frames in March or where they are to grow in mid-April or later. Thin out well. A well-drained sandy soil is best and a sunny position essential, for the flowers will not open properly in shade. Pick off dead flowers for continuous display.

Drosanthemum (*Aizoaceae*) Gay shrubby plants with small cylindrical to triangular leaves covered with sparkling raised dots. The rather small red or white flowers are very freely produced, and the plants are useful for bedding out. Max. W.T., 50°. P., seed, cuttings.

Echeveria (*Crassulaceae*) A large genus (with many synonyms!) of attractive rosette plants, sometimes on stems, which make large clumps quite quickly. Leaves often waxy or glaucous. The dainty urn-shaped flowers, red, orange, yellow or white, are carried along long stems. Most flower in summer, but some in winter. *E. secunda* and *E. glauca* are often used as carpet bedding plants. All are attractive; recommended are *E. agavoides, perelegans, gigantea* (nearly 2 ft. across), *setosa* and *carnicolor*. Best kept under glass are *E. Cotyledon, densiflora* and *farinosa*. They will grow in rooms, but the flowers may then dry up before opening. Max. W.T., 50°; cold frames will do for bedders, kept almost dry. P., seed, cuttings of almost any part.

Echinocactus (*Cactaceae*) Another much-reduced 'type' genus, now with about 10 species; round or barrel-shaped, flattened at the top, covered with fearsome spines. The flowers are smallish, seldom produced in pots. *E. Grusonii* is common; it will grow to nearly 3 ft. across and has interlacing golden spikes up to 3 in. long. *E. ingens*, similar, may reach 4 ft. *E. horizonthalonius* is smaller and will produce its pink flowers even on young pot specimens. Rich soil preferred.

Echinocereus (*Cactaceae*) A large genus with soft fleshy stems up to 15 in. long and 1 to 3 in. thick, erect or prostrate, making spreading clumps. Some have spines, others

9. *Echinopsis Eyriesii* is one of the commonest cottage window plants in Europe. The large flowers are white.

69

none. The flowers, white, yellow, red or purple, are quite large. They are easy to grow and many are quite hardy. There is little to choose between the many attractive species. W.T., 33°–40°. Cuttings should be taken in late June and July.

Echinopsis (*Cactaceae*) (Fig. 9) Very common, especially in cottage windows in Europe. Usually small, round or cylindrical, rarely columnar; spiny, with marked ribs. Characteristically flower very freely even when young, with very large pink or white flowers of great beauty, with long tubes. Many hybrids exist. Occasional sports occur which produce myriads of offsets; these plants seldom flower. Easy to grow; many fairly hardy.

Epiphyllum (*Cactaceae*) (Fig. 10) Shrubby epiphytes with flat or 3-angled leaf-like joints, often notched,

10. A hybrid *Epiphyllum*. These plants have flowers in a great variety of colours, and are often referred to as Orchid Cacti, or *Phyllocactus*.

seldom spiny. In the species the flowers are usually small and open at night; it is the hybrids, often crosses with *Heliocereus* or the *Hylocereus* tribe, and commonly called *Phyllocactus* or Orchid Cacti, which are best-known, with very beautiful flowers of almost every colour except blue. Often grafted on *Hylocereus undatus*. They like rich but porous soil with leaf-mould and old cow manure, half-shade, plenty of water when growing, fairly dry when not. Watering should be reduced for a few weeks after flowering. They appreciate plenty of air in summer and, unlike most succulents, a damp atmosphere obtained by regular syringeing. Hence they are more suitable for a mixed greenhouse than with other succulents.

Eriocereus (*Cactaceae*) Plants with long, thin, rather weak stems which usually sprawl and branch, with fairly long spines. The flowers are white and nocturnal, with a long tube. Among several good species *E. Martinii* is excellent, producing 8-in. flowers all summer. *E. Guelichii* has 10-in. flowers. Easy to grow in rather heavy soil. Prefer some shade. Good stock for grafting, often used for *Lobivia* and *Rebutia*. This genus is sometimes included in *Harrisia,* the species of which are weaker in growth and much more tender.

Euphorbia (*Euphorbiaceae*) (Fig. 11) This is one of the largest genera of plants and includes many diverse succulent forms. Many make tree-like growth, and many resemble cacti, apart from the flowers, which are usually insignificant. It is difficult to make a selection from at least 100 succulent species. Some are more woody than succulent, like the brilliant red-flowered *E. splendens*.

71

Other woody species, with leaves, are *E. Bojeri, alci-cornis, canariensis, lophogona*—the latter with white leaves and red stalks.

Among the cactiform are the jointed, 4-angled *E. abyssinica* and *E. similis*; 3-winged, fierce-spined *E. grandicornis*; and square-stemmed *E. resinifera*. *E. horrida* is like a spherical cactus. *E. Caput-Medusae* has radiating branches from a central head. There is a tuber-ous-rooted group, including *E. aequoris*, almost totally buried, and *E. namibensis* with parsnip-like root and many short, bristly branches. Of most interest, perhaps, are the very fleshy forms, such as the commonly seen *E. obesa,* spherical to sausage-shaped, which has male and female forms. The prominently ribbed *E. meloformis* re-sembles an *Astrophytum*. *E. bupleurifolia* is an example

11. The Euphor-bias are a very large and vari-able group. 1. *E. resinifera*; 2. *E. splendens*; 3. *E. obesa* (male plant); 4. *E. grandicornis*.

72

of a type which is covered with scales, which are in fact leaf-cushions, and has a few long narrow leaves on top.

In fact, the Euphorbias should be in any collection, and are a perfect subject for a specialized one. They are mainly easy to grow, needing a max. W.T. of 50°, and do well in rooms. The leafy forms are rich feeders and like much water in summer; the really succulent ones need special care with drainage and watering—usually no water in winter. P., seed, cuttings. Caution—the typical milky juice (latex) is poisonous and must be kept from eye, mouth or any cut.

Faucaria (*Aizoaceae*) (Fig. 17) Small clump-forming plants with 1 to 3 pairs of thick, triangular leaves, which have teeth or spines on the edges—hence the apt name Tiger's-jaw. The large yellow flowers appear in autumn. Easy to grow, good in rooms. Max. W.T., 55°. R., spring and summer. Free watering in winter, sparingly in summer. P., best from seed, also cuttings.

Fenestraria (*Aizoaceae*) Difficult but interesting; a 'window-plant' (see p. 12), forming large clumps of leaves, about 1 in. long, round in section and thickening towards the flattish translucent top. In nature these are buried up to the top. The pale orange flowers are very large—up to 3 in. across—in the commonest species, *F. aurantiaca* (Fig. 5). Need bright position; compost mainly of sand. Min. W.T., 50°. R., September/October–February, when very little watering. Little water even in growing period. P., seed, or division of clump, but resents disturbance, including repotting.

Ferocactus (*Cactaceae*) Spherical to cylindrical plants, some becoming very large (e.g. *F. Diguettii,* 12 ft. high, 3 ft. across), with marked ribs, and a heavy array of long thick spines, often attractively coloured, the central one often hooked and sometimes 5 in. long. The flowers are relatively small but showy, red, yellow or violet. All are worth growing. They like heavy, rubbly compost, and should be watered cautiously.

Gasteria (*Liliaceae*) Typically with thick, tongue-like, pointed leaves in two ascending rows, sometimes spirally twisted when older; a few make rosettes. The leaves are often covered with white tubercles (e.g. *G. verrucosa*). The quite showy flowers are like those of *Aloe,* and culture is the same, though they dislike direct sunlight. *G. Neliae* is attractive, with horny edge and regular white flecks on bright green leaves. *G. acinacifolia* forms a rosette of white-spotted, foot-long leaves. Tough plants, useful in rooms. P., seed, offsets, leaf cuttings.

Gibbaeum (*Aizoaceae*) (Fig. 5) Interesting but difficult; very succulent plants with 1 or 2 pairs of leaves, making clumps. Some are roughly spherical (e.g. *G. album, G. pilosulum*); some egg-shaped (e.g. *G. dispar*); some have finger-shaped leaves, short and blunt in *G. perviride,* longer in *G. pubescens* and more angular in *G. Nelii. G. velutinum* makes flat, triangular leaves. Most are curious in that the leaves of a pair are of different sizes, and the division between them is oblique. Small white or pink flowers. Growing period varies from one species to another, mainly from winter to early summer; water moderately then, keep quite dry in R. Min. W.T., 50°. P., seed, cuttings.

74

Glottiphyllum (*Aizoaceae*) (Fig. 17) The name means 'tongue-leaf' and is apt. The leaves are usually longer than wide, but sometimes short and broad, thick, fleshy, irregular, very soft and waxy to touch, usually a bright green; they usually radiate at ground level from a number of stem-like growths. They flower freely with large yellow blooms. Little to choose between species except leaf-shape. Easy to grow. R., February–May, quite dry and cold. Moderate water in growing period. P., seed, but this is often not true; cuttings best.

Greenovia (*Crassulaceae*) Very similar to *Aeonium*, but always on short stems; culture the same. Rosettes which have flowered die. Few species: *G. Aizoon* has white-haired rosettes 2½ in. across. *G. aurea* makes cushions of large glaucous rosettes and *G. gracilis* has small rosettes, in each case like rosebuds. Good room plants. Max. W.T., 50°. R., late summer–winter, when rosettes close up; keep fairly dry. P., seed, quicker from cuttings.

Gymnocalycium (*Cactaceae*) (Fig. 14) Curious but attractive globular cacti, ranging from 1 in. to 12 in. across, but mainly small, with rounded ribs divided into low tubercles, each carrying a few smallish spines. Many species and hybrids, all decorative, with quite large white or pink flowers (red in *G. Baldianum*), usually freely produced and on young plants. *G. Mihanovichii* has reddish zones on the skin. Easy to grow; rich soil, much water in the summer. Many are fairly hardy. All of them prefer half-shade.

Haworthia (*Liliaceae*) Mainly rosette plants, some remaining low, some ascending, a few with leaves in two rows. Some have very hard, tubercled leaves, as *H. margaritifera* and *H. fasciata;* some are bristly (*H. altilinea*); others have soft, translucent, triangular leaves, such as *H. cymbiformis, H. planifolia* (Fig. 1), and the netted *H. tessellata.* In some fleshy forms the rosettes are, in nature, buried to expose only the flat leaf-ends, as with *H. retusa* and the most adapted forms, *H. Maughanii*—a little like *Fenestraria*—and *H. truncata,* with two rows of thick, flattened, crowded leaves. The long-stalked flowers are insignificant. Most are easy to grow and thrive in rooms, but the last two mentioned need treatment more as for *Lithops.* Otherwise culture as for *Aloe.* Max. W.T., 55°. R., winter, when water moderately. P., seed, offsets. Repot in late summer.

Heliocereus (*Cactaceae*) Usually trailers, with thin stems, and remarkable for their large, beautiful, strong-scented flowers, for which they are called the 'Sun Cacti'. These may be red, often with touches of green, purplish or white, and up to 6 in. long. *H. speciosus* is often seen, and is one of the parents of many of the hybrid *Epiphyllums* (*q.v.*). Like them these plants like heat, some air moisture, leafy soil and half-shade. A little bonemeal may be given. Min. W.T., 50°.

Hylocereus (*Cactaceae*) Epiphytic plants with aerial roots, sometimes in nature with no connection with the soil; stems long-jointed, notched, angular or winged, with few small spines. The usually nocturnal flowers, often scented, have white petals and red, purple or green sepals, are sometimes very freely produced, and are very large—usually 6 in. or 8 in. and sometimes 12 in. long.

The fruits are also large. They need warmth, air moisture and a free root-run to flower, and prefer very rich, leafy soil, without lime, and half-shade. *H. undatus* and *H. triangularis* are commonly seen, and are often used as grafting stocks for pendulous plants.

Kalanchoë (*Crassulaceae*) (Fig. 7) Closely related to *Bryophyllum*, but not producing adventitious buds. Erect, sub-shrubby plants, often becoming large, with fairly large opposite leaves and often large clusters of small bright flowers, white, red or yellow. The flower-bearing shoots die afterwards, but new growths arise at the base. *K. Blossfeldiana*, with scarlet flowers in winter and spring, is grown commercially, and *K. flammea* (orange-red) and *K. carnea* (pink) are equally good value. In others the leaves are the main attraction: *K. grandiflora* has bluish, rounded, notched leaves; *K. marmorata* greyish leaves of similar shape with handsome brown markings; *K. pruinosa* long, pointed, notched glaucous leaves; and *K. tomentosa* is covered with silvery fur, reddish-brown at the leaf-tips.

Easy to grow, usually good in rooms. The flowering kinds are grown rather like *Rochea coccinea*, being kept in shaded frames and cut back in late June. Max. W.T., 50°. P., seed, cuttings.

Kleinia (*Compositae*) (Fig. 12) A genus of several very interesting plants, most quite easy to grow in rooms. The most commonly seen is *K. articulata*, the 'Candle Plant', which has blue-grey, jointed stems and, for a short season, ivy-shaped leaves. *K. Anteuphorbium* has very long joints and lanceolate, silver-grey leaves. *K. ficoides* and

K. repens are more prostrate plants, with narrow leaves and rigid joints. *K. neriifolia,* which eventually makes a 10-ft. bush, looks like a miniature palm-tree. Most interesting is *K. gomphophylla,* which has prostrate stems rooting as they go, with leaves like green acorns. They have pale stripes which are in fact 'sun-windows'. This is

12. Two of the Candle Plants: left, *Kleinia tomentosa,* covered in close white felt; right, *K. articulata.*

a desert plant and needs less water than the others, but all need cautious watering, particularly *K. tomentosa,* a very attractive plant forming 12-in. clumps with cylindrical leaves, pointed at both ends, about 1½ in. long, the whole covered with close white felt. It is very sensitive to changes of temperature. Keep all kleinias nearly dry in summer.

Max. W.T., 50°. P., seed or cuttings; the joints, which are easily detached, root rapidly. Repot in early autumn.

Lampranthus (*Aizoaceae*) More or less shrubby plants,

with fairly distant leaves, usually long and narrow. They
flower freely during most of the summer, and are much
used for bedding, particularly in milder localities. They
are also attractive pot and basket plants. The nurseryman
will call most of them *Mesembryanthemum*. There are
very many attractive species, most with 2- or 3-in.
flowers. Among the pink ones are *L. blandus, roseus*
(Fig. 4) and *falciformis*; reds include scarlet *L. coccineus,*
purple-carmine *L. conspicuus*, purple-red *L. Haworthii*
and *L. spectabilis* (the latter three particularly striking).
L. Zeyheri is a brilliant violet-purple; *L. glaucus* a large
yellow; *L. aurantiacus* is orange, *L. tenuifolius* orange-
scarlet, *L. aureus* yellow or orange. All need only protection from frost and to be kept nearly dry in winter. They
can be overwintered in a light, airy room. P., seed,
quicker from cuttings.

Lemaireocereus (*Cactaceae*) Growing into tree-like
clumps, with stems 3 to 6 in. thick, and with short, often
coloured spines. Most branch freely, but *L. marginatus,*
often used as a hedge-plant in Mexico, grows straight up.
The ridges of its ribs are topped with wool. Flowers usually small; the species are prized more for their form and
colouring, especially good in seedlings. Culture as for
Cereus. Keep from cold.

Leuchtenbergia (*Cactaceae*) (Fig. 13) *L. principis*, the
only species, is a remarkable cactus with long root,
woody stem and very long triangular tubercles, 5 in. long
and $\frac{3}{8}$ in. across, with papery spines 4 in. long at the ends.
The yellow flower is $2\frac{1}{2}$ in. across. Easy to grow in porous
soil: much water while in growth. Seedlings grow fast.

13. *Leuchtenbergia principis,* a very unusual cactus. The tubercles are exceptionally long, and each has several long spines.

flowering in 4 or 5 years. Can be propagated by using tubercles as cuttings.

Lithops (*Aizoaceae*) (Fig. 5) A large genus of very fleshy plant-bodies, often coloured and patterned to resemble stones (see p. 52), and in nature buried up to the top, living in the hottest desert conditions. The bodies are conical or cylindrical, and the two leaves which compose each are completely joined, apart from a more or less pronounced cleft in the top. The yellow or white flowers appear in the cleft, and are usually bigger than the body; the top is flat or slightly convex.

The species are all basically similar, but vary in markings and size, the latter from about ⅜ in. to 1¾ in. in height. In cultivation they often exceed the natural size. It is best to grow them in separate pots and, since they like very hot sun, to sink the pots in a gravelly bed. This avoids root-scorch. Very sandy soil is necessary. Watering should always be cautious, and none given in winter. They can be grown on a sunny window-sill. Min. W.T., 45°. R., November/January–April/May. P., seeds; cuttings can also be used or clumps divided.

Lobivia (*Cactaceae*)   A large genus of small, round or cylindrical, ribbed, spiny plants, with relatively large flowers, usually red, sometimes white or yellow. Very free-flowering and easy to grow. Many hybrids exist. Prefer some shade and rich, porous, limy soil; cool in winter.

Lophocereus (*Cactaceae*)   The one species, *L. Schottii*, grows to 15 ft., about 2½ in. thick, with thick spines and many bristles. The flowers are small. It is the monstrous form, often labelled *Cereus* or *Lemaireocereus Mieckleyanus*, that is usually grown—an extraordinary sight with irregular ribs, quite spineless and smooth (Fig. 2). Water cautiously.

Lophophora (*Cactaceae*)   *L. Williamsii* is notorious as *mescal* or *peyotl*, the dried form in which it was eaten by the Mexican Indians, since it contains powerful intoxicating and narcotic alkaloids. Fairly easy to grow, it is one of a group (mainly difficult) of cacti which look more like round, grey, scaly potatoes, with low tubercles and wool-bearing areoles. There is a large tap-root. Flowers smallish, pink to white. Needs heavy, porous soil. Rather slow from seed.

Mammillaria (*Cactaceae*) (Fig. 14)   At least 240 species, mainly globular, sometimes cylindrical, all with tubercles, which have spines at the apex and often wool in the axils. Flowers smallish but attractive, usually in a ring round the top, followed by red fruits. There are too many —mostly attractive and easy to grow—to give any list of species. Good room plants. The genus is divided into two sections, one with watery sap and the other with milky sap (which may only be in the body and not the tubercles). The former need plenty of water in summer, the latter less. Many are very winter-hardy if dry.

14. Cacti with tubercles. Left, *Gymnocalycium multiflorum*; centre, *Mammillaria Schiedeana*; right, *M. longimamma* (sometimes called *Dolicothele longimamma*).

Mesembryanthemum (*Aizoaceae*) According to the latest authorities, very few species, if any, are left to this, the original genus of the family, and they are shrubby ones, such as *Lampranthus* and other genera listed on p. 50. Nurserymen, however, continue to use the name for many shrubby and the few annual species, and it is used loosely to denote any member of the tribe (Fig. 4).

Mitrophyllum (*Aizoaceae*) (Fig. 15) As rare as they are interesting, these plants have two different types of leaf

15. Members of the *Aizoaceae* with two different leaf forms. Above, *Mitrophyllum mitratum*; left, *Monilaria moniliformis*; right, *Cheiridopsis peculiaris*.

according to season. In the resting period the leaves are thick and cylindrical, splitting into a jaw shape at the top. At the onset of the growing season a pair of long, narrow leaves, joined only at the base, emerge from the 'stem' of the resting leaf. The new resting leaf eventually appears from between these. Flowers are rare. Best grown in pots in a gravel bed; very sandy soil; little water in growth period, none in R., October/November–August. Min. W.T., 50°. P., seed.

Monilaria (*Aizoaceae*) (Fig. 15)   The resting leaves are joined into round bodies; the growing-period leaves resemble a pair of antlers, curving up in a U-shape from the base. These sparkle with little raised dots. Culture as for *Mitrophyllum*. R., March–October.

Nananthus (*Aizoaceae*)   A genus of small succulents,

with 4 to 6 pairs of narrow, triangular leaves. The smallest is *N. Loganae*, with leaves about $\frac{7}{8}$ in. long and $\frac{1}{8}$ to $\frac{1}{3}$ in. wide. They are often dotted or warty, and some are glaucous, sometimes with reddish markings. The flowers are yellow, and in some species have a red line down each petal. As they have long, fleshy roots, deep narrow pots are necessary. Soil should be very sandy. Min. W.T., 50°. R., winter, quite dry. Water moderately in growth period. P., seed.

Notocactus (*Cactaceae*) Usually globular with flattened top, ribbed, spiny, up to 6 in. across; rarely cylindrical, as *N. Leninghausii*, 3 ft. tall, which is laced with golden bristles. Flowers prolific, up to 3 in. wide, usually smaller, mainly yellow. Good species include *N. concinnus, mammulosus, Ottonis, Scopa.* Fairly rich soil. Very hardy.

Ophthalmophyllum (*Aizoaceae*) (Fig. 5) Small plants, up to $1\frac{1}{2}$ in. high, very like *Lithops,* but with pronounced rounded lobes, often translucent. Flowers pink, reddish or white. Soil should be very sandy. Min. W.T., 50°. R., March–August, quite dry, even for seedlings. P., seed.

Opuntia (*Cactaceae*) (Figs. 2, 16) About 300 species, divided into four well-marked groups: *Platyopuntia,* the largest, with flattened round or oval joints; *Brasiliopuntia,* similar but with cylindrical main stem; *Tephrocactus,* with spherical or ovoid joints; and *Cylindropuntia,* with columnar stems or long cylindrical joints. Some have primitive, usually awl-shaped leaves which usually fall off soon (e.g. *O. subulata*). Most are spiny, the spines sometimes papery (*O. papyracantha*), but mainly stiff— 4 in. long in *O. aoracantha.* Always with glochids (tiny

16. **Different forms of Opuntias. Left,** *O. subulata,* **with short-lived leaves;** centre, *O. papyracantha,* **with papery spines;** right, *O. microdasys,* **spineless but with glochids in the areoles.**

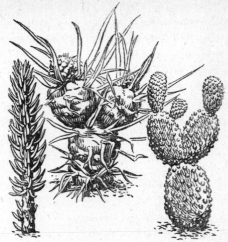

barbed bristles) in the areoles, which make the plants unpleasant to handle. Flowers usually large, of various shades of red, orange or yellow, and the fruits mainly large, egg- or pear-shaped, with areoles and spines, often sweet and edible—hence the name Prickly Pears. Mainly easy to grow in any limy, porous soil, very hardy if winter wet is kept off. A few are difficult. Many are too big and coarse for the small collection, but the small kinds are attractive. P., easy from joints.

Oscularia (*Aizoaceae*) Attractive shrubby plants with small greyish leaves, in *O. caulescens* with small teeth and in *O. deltoides* (Fig. 4) large ones. The small, prolific flowers are pink. Culture as for *Lampranthus.*

Pachyphytum (*Crassulaceae*) Attractive plants with

85

thick stems and leaves, usually rounded, ovate or spoon-shaped, purplish, greyish or with a white bloom. Like *Echeveria*, with similar flowers; culture the same, but unsuitable for bedding out.

Parodia (*Cactaceae*) Small globular or cylindrical plants, usually 2 or 3 in. through, with marked ribs and small tubercles, very spiny, usually woolly. Many flower very freely, with small red or yellow flowers; some are decorative with coloured spines and wool (e.g. yellow *P. chrysacanthion*). Attractive plants, very hardy. Culture as for *Notocactus*.

Pelargonium (*Geraniaceae*) Our familiar 'geraniums' are of course quite fleshy, and there are several desert forms. The leaves are similar to those of the bedding varieties, and drop in the R. period, which is usually summer. *P. gibbosum* has slender stems and swollen nodes; *P. tetragonum* has angular, jointed stems. *P. echinatum* is quite cactus-like with thorn-like growths. Others with short, much swollen stems are *P. carnosum. crassicaule* and *paradoxum*. The attractive flowers are white or pink. W.T., 55°. P., seed, cuttings.

Pereskia (*Cactaceae*) The most primitive cacti, barely succulent, very spiny, with woody stems, and large, glossy, flat, ovate, pointed leaves which may drop off in the rest period. Areoles large and woolly. The flowers are 1–3 in, across, usually in stalked clusters, white, yellow or pink, often scented, with leaf-like bracts. Fruit pear-shaped, sometimes edible. *P. aculeata Godseffiana* is most often grown, with white flowers and variegated leaves, purple on top, crimson below. Often used as stock for epiphytic cacti. Though rarely grown, they are attractive as well as curious. Need plenty of water and rich heavy loamy soil. Cuttings should be inserted without any drying off.

Pleiospilos (*Aizoaceae*) (Fig. 17)   Plants with 1-4 pairs of leaves, making clumps, the leaves usually roughly

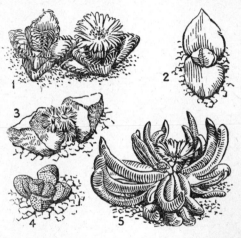

17. Another group of much-adapted *Aizoaceae*. 1. *Faucaria tigrina*; 2. *Pleiospilos simulans*; 3. *P. Bolusii*; 4. *Stomatium Logani*; 5. *Glottiphyllum* hybrid.

triangular and very thick, grey to brownish, with small dots, resembling pieces of granite. Flowers large, red or yellow, sometimes several together. *P. Bolusii* is often seen, with very broad, short leaves. *P. Nelii* has neat hemispherical leaves. All species are interesting. Prefer very sandy soil. Repot with caution. Min. W.T., 60°. R., January-September, quite dry. Water freely as leaves develop, then moderately. P., seed, division of clumps.

Portulaca (*Portulacaceae*) *P. grandiflora* is fairly well known as a half-hardy annual; it has radiating, prostrate stems with cylindrical leaves and bright flowers, which are red in the species, but in the garden hybrids are both single and double and of many colours. Culture as for *Dorotheanthus,* but is a little less hardy. Makes an attractive pot plant.

Rebutia (*Cactaceae*) Small, spiny plants, tubercled like *Mammillaria,* 1 or 2 in. across, popular for the freedom with which the small flowers, in a great range of colours, are produced, over a long period. *R. minuscula* is one of the smallest cacti, $1\frac{1}{2}$ in. across, 1 in. high with $1\frac{1}{2}$ in. flowers all spring and summer. Very easy to grow.

Rhipsalis (*Cactaceae*) Epiphytic plants from tropical forests, with cylindrical, flat or angular joints, and woolly bristly areoles. Growths often branching, prostrate or trailing, with aerial roots. Small starry flowers, white, pink, red or greenish, with few petals profusely produced in winter. Need overhead spraying and warm humid air conditions, little watering, rich, very humusy but porous soil, and much shade. Suitable for an orchid house, and will grow in orchid compost.

The *Rhipsalis* are noteworthy, being the only cactus genus native to Africa and Ceylon as well as America.

Rochea (*Crassulaceae*) *R. coccinea* is the florist's 'Crassula' (also known as *Kalosanthes*), with stems up to 2 ft. high, thin triangular leaves arranged crosswise and fairly closely packed, and showy tubular carmine flowers in terminal clusters. These appear in early spring if forced, later if not. There are other equally attractive species, in which the flowers may be white, pink, yellow or red. Easy plants, good in rooms. W.T., 40°–45°. P., seed, usually from cuttings (best in late spring).

Sedum (*Crassulaceae*) A genus of at least 500 species, mainly hardy, many commonly grown and a number native to Britain. Some of these can be grown in pots, but tend to grow too large. The tender kinds only are normally included in a greenhouse selection, and these are mainly Mexican, with a few from Madeira. They are all attractive plants, forming loose rosettes or spiral groups of leaves at the end of fleshy stems, and vary from several feet high to small prostrate plants. The leaves are of many shapes and may be green, red, bluish or whitish, and the flowers, usually small in clusters, are of many colours.

Among tall-growing species, which tend to grow straggly, are *S. Adolphii, dendroideum, Nussbaumeri, Treleasei* and *Weinbergii*, with large roughly boat-shaped leaves; *S. praealtum*, with long flat leaves; *S. Palmerii*, with flat, rounded leaves; and *S. compressum*, with leaves oblanceolate and flattish. Perhaps the most attractive are *S. allantoides, pachyphyllum* and *guatamalense*, the first two whitish, the latter purplish; *S. bellum*, with mealy-white, spoon-shaped leaves; and *S. farinosum*, with mealy, awl-shaped leaves. *S. Stahlii* is a small spreading plant with reddish, oval leaves $\frac{1}{2}$ in. long.

All are very easy to grow. Max. W.T., 50°. P., cuttings, division, usually easy from leaves.

Selenicereus (*Cactaceae*) Trailers or climbers with long, thin, ribbed, branching stems, usually with small spines and aerial roots. The flowers are immense, cup-shaped, around 8 in. long and across, on a long tube. They are white or tinged with red, purple, yellow or green, with radiating sepals and many stamens. Mainly night-flowering, fading before daybreak; often very sweetly scented. Old plants will flower over 2 or 3 months. They like a rich, humusy, limy soil, and need some warmth, much water and overhead sprays through spring and summer. *S. grandiflorus*—of which Prof. Borg rightly says, 'No collection of cacti should be without this marvel of the vegetable kingdom'—is called 'Queen of the Night', and they are all known as Moon Cacti.

Sempervivum (*Crassulaceae*) Rosette plants with long flower spikes with terminal clusters of flowers in many colours, not usually admitted as 'succulents' by the purist owing to their complete hardiness; but they make attractive pot plants for cool conditions. Many have nice red or purplish tints on the leaves and some are 'spider-webbed' (*S. arachnoideum*, etc.). Most plants in cultivation are hybrids. Porous soil; dry in winter. P., offsets.

Senecio (*Compositae*) The succulent members of this vast genus, which contains the familiar Groundsel, were once all included under *Kleinia*. Culture is identical and most are well worth growing. The adaptations to dry conditions vary a lot. At one extreme is *S. stapeliiformis,* with grey-green stems like a *Stapelia,* but with the typical reddish-orange flower of a weedy Composite—a species needing to be kept very dry. *S. fulgens* has a flask-shaped stem and a spiral bunch of round, flat, glaucous leaves, up to 4 in. long. Several form clumps of short stems and have prostrate branches, like *S. adenocalyx,* or runners, like *S. Klinghardtianus,* while *S. phonolithicus* has succulent branches up to 3 ft., with long, thin, curved leaves and a bright bunch of yellow flowers; *S. scaposus* and *S. vestita* have a large rosette of similar leaves, glaucous and partly white-felted.

Stapelia (*Asclepiadaceae*) (Fig. 18)   Many species and hybrids of low branching plants with fleshy, upright,

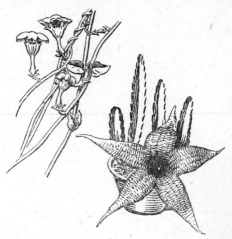

18. Two very different members of the *Asclepiadaceae.* Left, the climbing *Ceropegia Sandersonii;* right, *Stapelia gigantea,* with flowers 11 inches across.

quadrangular stems, toothed on the angles, with short-lived or no leaves. Remarkable for the bizarre, surrealist flowers, usually with a yellowish background more or less marked with brown, dark red or purple, often hairy and usually with a powerful carrion smell that attracts the blowflies that fertilize them—hence the name Carrion Flower. A few are odourless and one or two pleasantly scented. The flowers appear in mid-summer, and have a tube and a bell- or star-shaped corolla, more or less cut into 5 lobes, with a central fleshy ring (the corona). Some grow in clusters of up to 10, others singly or in pairs, and they vary from 1 to 11 in. across. The fruits are horn-shaped, two to a flower, appearing months later, and the seeds are equipped with parachutes. The medium-sized *S. variegata* is most often seen. Easy to grow, even indoors, preferring air moisture in summer and enjoying spraying on hot days. Rich, humus-containing, porous soil. Reduce watering towards autumn, keep fairly dry in winter. Max. W.T., 55°. P., seed, cuttings.

Stomatium (*Aizoaceae*) (Fig. 17) Small almost stemless plants with 2 or more pairs of leaves, usually about 3 times longer than broad, semi-circular or triangular in section, often with toothed upper edges. *S. suaveolens* is exceptional as its leaves are barely longer than broad. Flowers fairly small, yellow. Easy plants. Min. W.T., 45°. R., autumn-spring P., seed, cuttings.

Zygocactus (*Cactaceae*) Epiphytic, pendulous plants, much branched, with short, flat, notched, leaf-like joints. *Z. truncatus* is the only species, with flowers typically deep pink. The many hybrids are white, red, violet, etc. The flowers, 3 in. long and 1 in. across, are profusely produced in autumn and winter—hence the name Christmas Cactus—and last well. Treat like *Epiphyllum*, but much hardier. Often grafted on to columnar stock to make a 'standard', or may be grown in baskets.